D0231619

THE
MUNRO
ALMANAC
Cameron McNeish

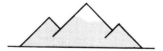

LOCHAR PUBLISHING · MOFFAT · SCOTLAND

Published by Lochar Publishing Ltd
Moffat DG10 9ED

British Library Cataloguing in Publication Data
McNeish, Cameron
  The munro almanac.
  1. Scotland. Highlands. Mountain Munros. Visitors'
  guides
  I. Title
  914.115

  ISBN 0–948403–59–4

First edition published April, 1991.
Reprinted June, 1991.

Typeset in 11 on 13pt Goudy Old Style by
Chapterhouse, Formby and printed in Scotland by
Eagle Colourbooks Ltd.

Maps by David Langworth

CONTENTS

INTRODUCTION

The Munros are the separate mountains over 3000 feet in Scotland. This book describes 277 such mountains, the 276 as contained in the 1981 edition of *Munro's Tables* (published by the Scottish Mountaineering Trust) plus the addition of Beinn Teallach in 1984.

Periodic revisions have taken place ever since Sir Hugh T. Munro, Bart, of Lindertis published his original list in 1891. In that list, published in the Scottish Mountaineering Club Journal, he claimed 538 tops over 3000 feet, 283 of which he believed merited status as 'separate mountains'. (There has always been much speculation about the criteria for deciding what separates a 'top' from a 'mountain'. In 1933, J. Gall Inglis then editor of *Munro's Tables*, suggested that there should be a drop of 75–100 feet between mountains but to date there has been no firm guideline on what constitutes a 'mountain'. Munro himself was in favour of updating only when maps were re-surveyed and revised.)

But almost immediately, the Ordnance Survey (OS) published their revised six-inch maps of Scotland and discrepancies were found in Munro's tabulations. Munro himself began a revision of his list but sadly died in 1919, aged sixty-three, before it was published. J. R. Young and A. W. Peacock, fellow members of the Scottish Mountaineering Club (SMC), took on the task and working from Munro's notes and card index eventually produced a revised Tables in 1921. This new list produced 276 separate mountains of over 3000 feet.

Various committees and editors of *Munro's Tables* have made alterations to the list since, based mainly on new surveys. Such alterations have not always gone without criticism. There is a strong lobby which insists that the *Munro's Tables* should remain faithful to the historical document which Sir Hugh Munro compiled, while others are happy to go along with the various additions and deletions which are thrown up now and again by the Ordnance Survey.

However, a major revision took place in 1981 at the hands of Hamish Brown and J. C. Donaldson when forty-seven of Munro's 'tops' were demoted and seven 'mountains' were dropped to 'top' status. In addition twenty-two new 'tops' were introduced and four 'tops' were promoted to 'mountain' status. This created some controversy at the time with one writer claiming that the changes had been made, 'solely at the whim of the editors'. It was felt that perhaps Munro would turn in his grave, as Carn Cloich-mhuillin in the Cairngorms, the mountain which he hoped to climb as his final 3000-footer, had been demoted in the 'incomprehensible' Brown/Donaldson revisions.

But such are the emotions stirred by the Munros. In 1974 metrication was adopted and metric heights appeared side by side with the more familiar imperial heights, but in the 1981 revision the imperial figures were removed. This also caused some consternation and there were fears that the Munros would be relegated to those mountains which reached the 1000-metre plumbline. These fears were proved false but there is still a reluctance to refer to a Munro as 'a mountain of over 914 metres'.

Sir Hugh Munro never completed his round, he died before climbing the Inaccessible Pinnacle in the Cuillin and the above mentioned Carn Cloich-mhuillin. In 1901 the Revd. A. E. Robertson completed the first ascent of all 283 mountains and another cleric, the Revd. A. R. G. Burn became the first person to climb all the Munros and Tops in 1923.

Surprisingly in view of the numbers crawling round the Munros today, it wasn't until 1971 that the number of Munroists (those who have climbed all the 3000 feet 'mountains') reached 100. Hundreds more have become members of this once élite band since and today the activity known as Munro-bagging is a popular and growing aspect of Scottish mountaineering.

The Scottish Mountaineering Club keep a list of those who have 'compleated' (*sic*) the round of Munros and the present 'keeper' of those records is Bill Brooker, 25 Deeview Road South, Cults, Aberdeen, Grampian Region AB1 9NA.

While the SMC doesn't officially keep 'records' of the quickest rounds, the fastest to date goes to a fell

Gulvain

runner, Mark Elsegood who climbed all 277 Munros in a remarkable sixty-six days in 1988. In 1974 Hamish Brown became the first person to climb all the mountains in one expedition, in 1984–85. Martin Moran climbed them all during the months of the winter equinox, and in 1979 Kathy Murgatroyd became the first woman to climb them all in one trip. They have been climbed on mountain bike, (or while carrying a mountain bike) and others have attempted to climb them all on skis.

Notes on using this book
While the *Munro's Tables* offer lists of the Munros and the Tops, not to forget the Corbetts, those hills which reach the 2500 feet contour and the *Donald's Tables* of those lowland hills which top 2000 feet; and while other guide books, including the *Munro's Tables* companion volume, *The Munros*, offer details

of the routes on the mountains, I wanted to put together a work which offered as much information as possible about the Munros in one small book.

Each section contains information on accommodation, public transport to and within the section area, the height and grid reference of each summit, the meaning and pronunciation of each mountain and details of the most straightforward ascent, including approximate times, distances and ascent climbed.

Contour line measurements in the route description are given in metres in line with the most recent 1:50 000 Ordnance Survey (OS) maps. For distances on the hill both miles and kilometres are quoted as well as feet and metres as appropriate.

The route descriptions are not meant to give a step by step account of how to climb the mountain, but only a very rough outline of what I have found to be the best route of ascent. Many will disagree with some of the recommended routes, but I have tried to balance the need for longer multi-top expeditions with shorter day trips. No one climbs the Munros at the rate of one mountain per day, and there is a great satisfaction to be had in walking the likes of the South Glen Shiel Ridge when you can traverse seven Munros in a day. Likewise there will be those capable of walking the likes of the Cuillin Ridge in one day, while I have broken it up into four expeditions.

These descriptions should only be used as a guide, in conjunction with the appropriate Ordnance Survey (OS) map.

Access
It has always been understood that in Scotland the hillwalker or mountaineer has enjoyed a moral right of freedom-to-roam in wild places, provided that is accompanied by good countryside manners and respect for those other activities which make use of wild areas, i.e. grouse shooting and deer stalking. This *de facto* freedom to roam must be safeguarded for sadly, there is a growing number of landowners who are worried about the increased numbers of walkers on the hills and who are anxious to see a change in the law regarding access.

Ciste Duibhe and Sgurr na Ceathreamhnan

In short, the law at present says a trespass has been committed by a person who goes on to land owned or occupied by another without that person's consent and without having a right to do so. But a simple trespass is not enshrined in statute as a criminal offence, so there can't be a prosecution. The owner or occupier of the property must either obtain interdict, (i.e. a court ruling that the trespass must not happen again), or, if damage to property has occurred, to raise an action for damages. Additionally, a 'trespasser' may be asked by the owner or occupier to leave the property and in the event of that person refusing to leave, the owner or occupier has the right to use 'reasonable force' to make him leave. There is no further definition as to reasonable force.

However, there is a widely held public acceptance that walkers and climbers are more or less free to roam the upland areas of Scotland without undue restriction, and any impingement on that 'moral right' would undoubtedly create public outcry. At the time of writing the Scottish Landowners Federation is very keen to create a dialogue with walking and mountaineering organisations in a search for mutual understanding and tolerance. Most estates in the Highlands are involved in deer stalking and ask hill-goers to respect the stag-shooting season which runs from 20 August to 20 October. During this time there are many areas which are not affected by stalking, like those areas owned by the National Trust for Scotland (NTS) and many Nature Conservancy Council (NCC) reserves. I have listed local telephone numbers of estates, however, so that you can find out for yourself where stalking is taking place. Often a chat with the gamekeeper or factor will result in a good compromise with the shooters chasing their deer on one side of the estate and the Munro-bagger enjoying his or her walk on the other.

Bear in mind though that estates earn a large part of their annual income from stalking, and there often has to be compromise. The alternative to stalking on many estates could well be something more unpleasant, like mass conifer afforestation. Dialogue and mutual respect and understanding is the only way forward.

1 BEN LOMOND AND THE ARROCHAR ALPS

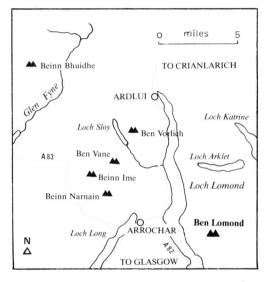

Suggested Base:	Arrochar
Accommodation:	Hotels, guest houses and b/b at Arrochar, Ardlui, Cairndow, Inveraray, Lochgoilhead and Tarbet. Youth Hostels at Arrochar (Ardgarten), Balloch, Inveraray, Loch Ard, Inverbeg and Rowardennan. Camping/Caravan sites at Ardgarten, Ardlui, Arrochar, Balloch, Balmaha, Inveraray and Luss.

Public Transport: Rail: London to Fort William
and Glasgow to Oban and Fort
William. Stations at Arrochar
and Ardlui. There is also a train
line from Glasgow to Balloch on
Loch Lomondside. Buses:
Balmaha, Arrochar, Glen Croe,
Glen Kinglas, Cairndow, Loch
Shira and Aberfoyle can all be
reached by bus from Glasgow.

Ben Lomond

Mountain: Ben Lomond 3195 ft/974 m

Map: OS Sheet 56: GR 367029
Translation: Beacon Hill
Pronunciation: Low-mond
Access Point: Rowardennan Hotel, GR 360983
Distance: 7 miles/3195 ft; 11.2 km/974 m ascent
Approx Time: 4–6 hours
Route: Follow path through trees from
Rowardennan Hotel to lower slopes of south ridge.
Follow obvious path along broad middle ridge to
summit cone where the path zig-zags to summit ridge.
A few bumps in the ridge lead to the summit.
Stalking Information: National Trust for Scotland
property. No problems.

Mountain: Beinn Narnain and Beinn Ime
3038 ft/926 m and 3316 ft/1011 m

Map: OS Sheet 56: GR 272067 and GR 255085
Translation: unknown and butter hill
Pronunciation: as spelt
Access Point: A83 at Loch Long, GR 294050
Distance: 7 miles/4000 ft; 11.2 km/1219 m ascent
Approx Time: 5–7 hours
Route: Start near turn off to Succoth Farm. Follow
path steeply uphill through forest to open hill.
Continue NW up broad ridge to the knoll of Cruach
nam Miseag. Follow faint path through rock to the
Spearhead, a rock prow which lies on the ridge.
Climb a short gully on its right to summit plateau of
Beinn Narnain. Continue to Beinn Ime by way of
Bealach a Mhaim then climb NNW slopes to summit
trig point
Stalking Information: No restrictions.

Mountain: Ben Vane 3002/915 m

Map: OS Sheet 56: GR 278098
Translation: Middle Hill
Pronunciation: as spelt
Access Point: Inveruglas, Loch Lomondside
Distance: 7 miles/3000 ft; 11.2 km/914 m ascent
Approx Time: 4–6 hours
Route: Follow Hydro Board track to Coiregrogain
for just over a mile and then take the ESE ridge of the
hill. Higher up the ridge you'll have to thread your
way through some rocky and slabby outcrops but no
real difficulty.
Stalking Information: No restrictions.
NB: Parking at the foot of the Hydro Board road is
discouraged. Park opposite Loch Sloy Power Station
to the north.

Mountain: Ben Vorlich 3094 ft/943 m

Map: OS Sheets 56 and 50: GR 295124
Translation: hill of the bay

Pronunciation: as spelt
Access Point: Ardlui Station, GR 318154
Distance: 6 miles/3020 ft; 9.6 km/902 m ascent
Approx Time: 4–6 hours
Route: Take the second railway underpass to the south of Ardlui Station and take heather slopes to Coire Creagach. Climb on the NW side of the stream to the upper corrie where the main ridge will be reached NNE of the summit.
Stalking Information: No restrictions.

Mountain: Beinn Bhuidhe 3110 ft/948 m

Map: OS Sheet 50: GR 204187
Translation: yellow hill
Pronunciation: Ben Boo-ie
Access Point: Glen Fyne, GR 228160
Distance: 6 miles/3100 ft; 9.6 km/945 m ascent
Approx Time: 5–7 hours
Route: Park beyond Glenfyne Lodge at the bridge near the Power Station. Continue on foot to Inverchorachan, then take to the slopes due west. Follow the south bank of the stream to its source then bear NW up steep grass and bracken into the upper corrie. Climb one of the gullies to the ridge. The summit cone is about half way along the ridge.
Stalking Information: Ardkinglas Estate Office. Tel: Cairndow 217.

2 THE CRIANLARICH HILLS

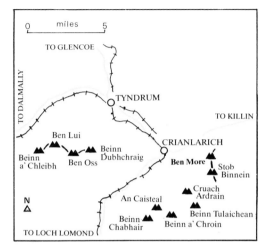

Suggested Base:	Crianlarich
Accommodation:	Hotels, guest houses and b/b at Crianlarich and Tyndrum. Youth Hostel at Crianlarich. Caravan site at Tyndrum and camping/caravan site in Glendochart.
Public Transport:	Rail: Crianlarich and Tyndrum are on the West Highland Line, London/Glasgow to Fort William. Also Glasgow to Oban line. Buses: Glasgow to Fort William or Oban for Crianlarich or Tyndrum.

Mountain: Beinn Chabhair, 3061 ft/933 m

Map: OS Sheets 50 and 56: GR 367180
Translation: possibly hill of the hawk
Pronunciation: Chavar
Access Point: Beinglas, GR 319188
Distance: 8 miles/2850 ft; 12.8 km/869 m ascent
Approx Time: 4–5 hours
Route: Climb steeply behind Beinglas Farm to above the falls of the Ben Glas Burn. Follow the burn to Lochan Beinn Chabhair then climb diagonally NE to the NW ridge. Follow ridge to summit.
Stalking Information: Glen Falloch Estate. Tel: Inveruglas 229.

Mountain: An Caisteal, 3264 ft/995 m and Beinn a'Chroin, 3084 ft/940 m

---

Map: OS Sheets 50 and 56: GR 379193 and GR 394186
Translation: the castle, hill of danger
Pronunciation: An Castail, Ben a Kroin
Access Point: Glen Falloch, GR 368238
Distance: 9 miles/2600 ft; 14.4 km/792 m ascent
Approx Time: 4–6 hours
Route: Follow rough track under railway, over the river by a bridge and up its west bank. Climb slopes of Sron Garbh and follow the ridge, Twistin' Hill to An Caisteal. Descend SSE ridge to col and climb rocky NW end of Beinn a'Chroin's summit ridge. Continue along crest to summit.
Stalking Information: Glen Falloch Estate. Tel: Inveruglas 229.

Mountain: Cruach Ardrain, 3431 ft/1046 m and Beinn Tulaichean, 3104 ft/946 m

---

Map: OS Sheets: 50, 51, 56 and 57: GR 409211 and GR 416196
Translation: stack of the high part and hill of the hillocks
Pronunciation: Kroo-ach ardrain, too-leach-an
Access Point: A82 road just south of Crianlarich

Distance: 9 miles/3500 ft; 14.4 km/1067 m ascent
Approx Time: 5–7 hours
Route: Cross bridge over railway to gain access to
forest. Go right, then left through a large clearing
following a path. Reach a broken fence after a short
distance, go uphill following the fence posts until you
reach the open hillside. Turn SE up the NW ridge to
Grey Height, then Meall Dhamh. Follow path
downhill, across a col and then steeply up to Cruach
Ardrain. To continue south to Tulaichean return SW
past two cairns and descend to a grassy ridge. Follow
crest of this ridge south to Beinn Tulaichean.
Stalking Information: No restrictions.
NB: Beinn Tulaichean can also be climbed from
Inverlochlarig in the south.

Mountain: Ben More, 3852 ft/1174 m and Stob
Binnein, 3822 ft/1165 m

Map: OS Sheet: 51: GR 432244 and GR 434226
Translation: big hill, hill of the anvil
Pronunciation: stobinyan
Access Point: Benmore Farm, GR 414257
Distance: 9 miles/5165 ft; 14.4 km/1574 m ascent
Approx Time: 6–8 hours
Route: Leave the farm and bear right towards the
ridge of Sron nam Forsairean. Follow this to the
summit. A hanging corrie, immediately below the
summit facing NW has a steep upper section which is
liable to avalanche in snowy conditions. This is the
site of several fatalities so avoid it if you can. Descend
south from Ben More, then SW following an
indistinct ridge to the flat Bealach-eader-dha Beinn.
Climb Stob Binnein from here by its north ridge.
Stalking Information: Forestry Commission. Tel:
Dalmally 254 and 301.

3 THE TYNDRUM HILLS

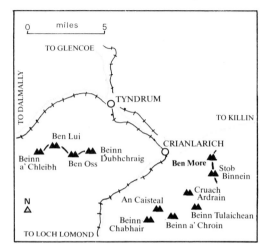

Suggested Base:	Tyndrum
Accommodation:	Hotels, guest houses and b/b in Tyndrum, Crianlarich and Bridge of Orchy. Youth Hostel at Crianlarich and private bunk house at Bridge of Orchy. Caravan site at Tyndrum.
Public Transport:	Rail: Tyndrum is on West Highland Line, London to Fort William, and the Glasgow–Oban line. Buses: Glasgow to Fort William or Glasgow to Oban.

***Mountain*:** Beinn a'Chleibh and Ben Lui,
3005 ft/916 m, 3707 ft/1130 m

***Map*:** OS Sheet 50: GR 251256, GR 266263
***Translation*:** hill of the chest, hill of the calf
***Pronunciation*:** Chlayv, Loo-ie
***Access Point*:** Glen Lochay, GR 239278
***Distance*:** 7 miles/3300 ft; 11.2 km/1006 m ascent
***Approx Time*:** 4–7 hours
***Route*:** Start at access point and cross River Lochay
by stepping stones. Follow path on the east side of the
Eas Daimh through conifer forest. After quarter of a
mile cross the burn and follow the path to the stile in
the fence which leads to open hillside. Climb NNW
ridge of Ben Lui to summit. Descend SW to the
bealach at the head of Fionn Choirein and follow flat
ridge to the summit of Beinn a'Chleibh.
***Stalking Information*:** Forestry Commission. Tel:
Dalmally 254 or 301.

***Mountain*:** Ben Oss and Beinn Dubhcraig,
3373 ft/1028 m, 3205 ft/977 m

***Map*:** OS Sheet 50: GR 287253, GR 308255
***Translation*:** loch outlet hill, black rock hill
***Pronunciation*:** doo-craig
***Access Point*:** Dailrigh, GR 344290
***Distance*:** 12 miles/3300 ft; 19.2 km/1006 m ascent
***Approx Time*:** 4–7 hours
***Route*:** Leave Dailrigh in Strathfillan. Follow rough
road on south side of river to a bridge over the
railway. Head west and cross the Allt Coire
Dubhcraig. Follow path through woods to open
hillside and continue SW up grassy corrie to the
shoulder of Beinn Dubhcraig. Follow broad stony
ridge to summit. From Dubhcraig follow ridge NW
and West to Ben Oss.
***Stalking Information*:** Glen Falloch Estate, D.
Neilson. Tel: Inveruglas 229.

4 CRIEFF AND LOCH EARN HILLS

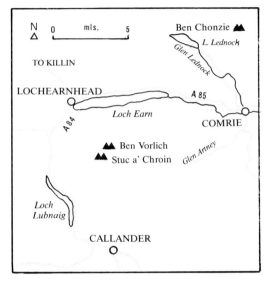

Suggested Base:	St Fillans or Comrie
Accommodation:	Hotels, guest houses and b/b at Callander, Comrie, Crieff, Lochearnhead, St Fillans and Strathyre. Camping sites at Callander and Crieff. Caravan/camping at Comrie.
Public Transport:	Rail: London, Glasgow and Edinburgh to Inverness. Connecting buses from stations at Perth and Stirling. Buses: Stirling to Crieff for ongoing connections. Both Crieff and Comrie can be reached by bus from Perth.

Mountain: Ben Vorlich and Stuc a'Chroin,
3232 ft/985 m and 3199 ft/975m

Map: OS Sheets 51 and 57: GR 629189 and GR 617175
Translation: hill of the bay, peak of danger
Pronunciation: stook a kroin
Access Point: Ardvorlich, GR 633232
Distance: 10 miles/3800ft; 16 km/1158 m ascent
Approx Time: 4–6 hours
Route: Take the private road from Ardvorlich House
south on to the open hillside in Glen Vorlich. Follow
the track to foot of Coire Buidhe and take SE side of
the corrie to reach the NNE ridge of Ben Vorlich and
to the summit. From the summit follow the line of
fence posts down to the Bealach an Dubh Choirein
and take steep boulder slope and zig-zag path
immediately right (NW) of the obvious buttress.
Good scrambling. Reach cairn at top of buttress and
head south to summit of Stuc a'Chroin.
Stalking Information: Ardvorlich Estate. Tel: St
Fillans 260.

Mountain: Ben Chonzie, 3054 ft/931 m

Map: OS Sheets 51 and 52: GR 774309
Translation: possibly hill of moss
Pronunciation: ben ee hoan; locally honzee
Access Point: Invergeldie, GR 743272
Distance: 8 miles/2200 ft; 12.8 km/671 m ascent
Approx Time: 3–5 hours
Route: From Invergeldie in Glen Lednock take the
right of way up the west side of the burn. At a track
junction just beyond a gate take the right hand track
and follow it across the burn and ENE up the hillside
then NE to broad summit ridge. A fence can then be
followed NW then NE to summit.
Stalking Information: Invergeldie Estate. Tel:
Comrie 619 or 240.

5 RANNOCH AND GLEN LYON

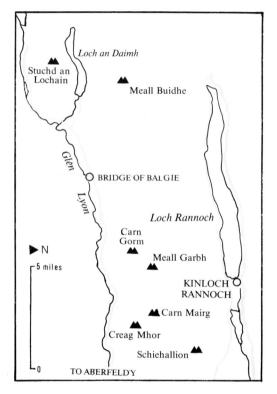

Loch an Daimh

Stuchd an Lochain

Meall Buidhe

Glen

Lyon

BRIDGE OF BALGIE

Loch Rannoch

Carn Gorm

Meall Garbh

KINLOCH RANNOCH

▶ N

5 miles

Carn Mairg

Creag Mhor

Schiehallion

0

TO ABERFELDY

Suggested Base:	Aberfeldy
Accommodation:	Hotels, guest houses and b/b at Fortingall, Kinloch Rannoch, Kenmore and Aberfeldy. Youth Hostel at Killin. Camping/Caravan sites at Kenmore, Kinloch Rannoch, Tummel Bridge and Aberfeldy.

Public Transport:	Rail: London, Glasgow and Edinburgh to Inverness. Stations at Perth, Dunkeld and Pitlochry for ongoing buses. Rannoch Station on West Highland Line for ongoing post bus. Buses: Perth and Pitlochry to Aberfeldy, Pitlochry to Kinloch Rannoch. Post Buses: Aberfeldy to Lubreoch in Glen Lyon, Kinloch Rannoch to Rannoch Station.

Mountain: Schiehallion 3553 ft/1083 m

Map: OS Sheet 51: GR 714548
Translation: Fairy Hill of the Caledonians
Pronunciation: Shee-hallian
Access Point: Braes of Foss, GR 750559
Distance: 5 miles/2470 ft; 8 km/753 m ascent
Approx Time: 3–5 hours
Route: Leave the car park and follow the path WSW across the moorland to join a track coming from Braes of Foss. This track divides but keep heading west towards the mountain. The path is over peaty ground and erosion is severe. Higher up things improve and the ground is stony. Continue on east ridge to summit.
Stalking Information: Kynachan Estate. Tel. Tummelbridge 209.

Mountain: Carn Gorm, 3373 ft/1028 m, Meall Garbh, 3176 ft/968 m, Carn Mairg, 3415 ft/1041 m, Creag Mhor, 3218 ft/981 m

Map: OS Sheet 51: GR 635501, GR 646517, GR 684513, GR 695496
Translation: Blue hill, rough hill, hill of sorrow or boundary hill, big rock
Pronunciation: as spelt
Access Point: Invervar, GR 666483
Distance: 11 miles/4550 ft; 17.6 km/1387 m ascent

Approx Time: 6–8 hours
Route: To co-operate with the landowner please walk this route in a *clockwise* direction. Follow the Invervar Burn to the 304.8 metres contour where its western tributary should be followed. Follow steep grassy slopes to summit of Carn Gorm. Follow broad ridge NNE to An Sgor and the summit of Meall Garbh. Follow the march fence to Meall a'Bharr then east and SE over uninteresting terrain to Carn Mairg. Follow ridge east of summit to Meall Liath then south on a wide grassy ridge around the head of Gleann Muillin to Creag Mhor.
Stalking Information: North Chesthill Estate. Tel: Glen Lyon 207.

Mountain: Stuchd an Lochain, 3150 ft/960 m and Meall Buidhe, 3058 ft/932 m

Map: OS Sheet 51: GR 483448 and GR 498499
Translation: peak of the small loch, yellow hill
Pronunciation: stoochk an lochan
Access Point: Loch an Daimh, GR 510436
Distance: 10 miles/3500 ft; 16 km/1067 m ascent
Approx Time: 5–8 hours
Route: Pass the south end of the dam and climb the steep grassy hillside south to reach the ridge above Coire Ban. Follow fence posts west to Creag an Fheadain, then SSW to Sron Chona Choirein then west and NW to summit of Stuchd an Lochain. Return to the dam. For Meall Buidhe cross to the north end of the dam and climb due north up easy slopes to Meal a'Phuill. Continue west then NNW along the broad ridge to the summit.
Stalking Information: Lochs Estate. Tel: Bridge of Balgie 224.

6 THE LAWERS GROUP

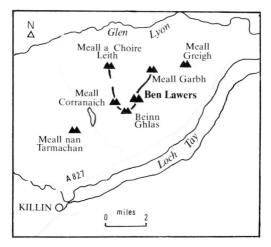

Suggested Base:	Killin
Accommodation:	Hotels, guest houses and b/b in Killin, Kenmore, Lochearnhead, Fortingall, and Aberfeldy. Youth Hostel at Killin. Camping/caravan sites at Glendochart and Kenmore. Caravan site at Killin.
Public Transport:	Rail: Glasgow to Stirling and Perth for ongoing buses. Also Glasgow to Crianlarich with ongoing bus connections. Buses: Stirling to Killin, Perth to Aberfeldy for ongoing post buses. Post Buses: Aberfeldy to Killin and Crianlarich to Killin.

Mountain: Meall Corranaich, 3507 ft/1069 m, Meall a'Choire Leith, 3038 ft/926 m

Map: OS Sheet 51: GR 616410, GR 612439
Translation: notched hill or hill of lamenting, hill of the grey corrie
Pronunciation: myowl koraneech, myowl kora lay
Access Point: Summit of Lochan na Lairige Road
Distance: 8 miles/2350 ft; 12.8 km/716 m ascent
Approx Time: 4–6 hours
Route: Leave road just north of Lochan and cross rough moorland SE over peat hags. Reach the Allt Gleann Da-Eig and follow it uphill to SW ridge of Meall Corranaich. Leave the summit and head north down the easy angled ridge. Keep to the NNE ridge, drop to a col then follow ridge on the flat topped summit plateau of Meall a'Choire Leith.
Stalking Information: Roro Estate. Tel: D. Campbell, Bridge of Balgie, 216.

Mountain: Beinn Ghlas, 3619 ft/1103 m, Ben Lawers, 3983 ft/1214 m, Meall Garbh, 3668 ft/1118 m, Meall Greigh, 3284 ft/1001 m

Map: OS Sheet 51: GR 626404, GR 636414, GR 644437, GR 674437
Translation: Green/grey hill, possibly loud hill or hoofed hill, rough hill, hill of the horse studs
Pronunciation: ben glas, ben lors, myowl garv, myowl gray
Access Point: Lawers on A827
Distance: 12 miles/5750 ft; 19.2 km/1753 m ascent
Approx Time: 7–10 hours
Route: Take private road to Machuim Farm. Beyond the farm follow track east of the Lawers Burn. Climb due north to Meall Greigh on easy grassy slopes. Follow west ridge to Meall Garbh. This ridge is broad and featureless and navigation can be tricky in misty weather. Follow ridge around the head of Coire na Cat over the subsidiary tops of An Stuc and Creag an Fhithich to steep slopes which lead to Ben Lawers. From summit follow east ridge down to Beinn Ghlas then obvious footpath which leads SW to the

National Trust for Scotland centre. Follow public
road back to A827 at Erdamucky.
Stalking Information: National Trust for Scotland.
No restrictions.

Mountain: Meall nan Tarmachan, 3422 ft/1043 m

Map: OS Sheet 51: GR585390
Translation: hill of the ptarmigan
Pronunciation: myowl nan taramachan
Access Point: Bridge over Allt a'Mhoirneas,
GR 603382
Distance: 8 miles/2440 ft; 12.8 km/744 m ascent
Approx Time: 4–6 hours
Route: Leave the bridge and follow a track beneath a
broad ridge. Climb easy grass slopes to a knoll on the
914.4 metres contour. Turn NW and climb various
terraces to the summit of Meall nan Tarmachan. It's
well worthwhile following the rest of the Tarmachan
ridge westwards before leaving Creag na Caillich by
its south ridge, then east and back to the track which
leads to the starting point.
Stalking Information: Boreland Estate. Tel: T. Frost,
Killin 562.

7 THE MAMLORN HILLS

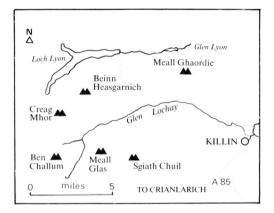

Suggested Base:	Killin
Accommodation:	Hotels, guest houses, b/b in Killin, Kenmore, Lochearnhead, Fortingall and Aberfeldy. Youth Hostels at Killin and Crianlarich. Camping/caravan sites at Glendochart and Kenmore. Caravan site at Killin.
Public Transport:	Rail: Glasgow to Stirling and Perth for ongoing buses. Also Glasgow to Crianlarich with ongoing bus connection to Killin. Buses: Stirling to Killin, Perth to Aberfeldy for ongoing post buses. Post Buses: Aberfeldy to Killin and Crianlarich to Killin.

Mountain: Meall Ghaordie, 3409 ft / 1039 m

Map: OS Sheet 51: GR 514397
Translation: Possibly rounded hill of the shoulder, arm, hand
Pronunciation: myowl girday
Access Point: Tullich in Glen Lochay, GR 516369
Distance: 4 miles/2700 ft; 6.4 km/823 m ascent
Approx Time: 3-5 hours
Route: From near the farm of Tullich climb easy though fairly uninteresting slopes in a north then NW direction. Pass some small rock outcrops and reach the summit soon afterwards. The OS trig point stands inside a circular cairn.
Stalking Information: Boreland Estate. Tel: Killin 339.

Mountain: Creag Mhor, Beinn Heasgarnich,
3438 ft / 1048 m, 3530 ft / 1076 m

Map: OS Sheets 50 and 51: GR 390361, and GR 413383
Translation: big rock, sheltered hill
Pronunciation: craig vore, heskarneech
Access Point: Badour in Glen Lochay, GR 431351
Distance: 10 miles/4000 ft; 16 km/1219 m ascent
Approx Time: 5-8 hours
Route: Leave the cottage of Badour and follow grassy slopes in a NW direction making for the top of Stob an Fhir-bhogha. A broad ridge leads north and over two slight bumps to the summit hump of Beinn Heasgarnich. Return to Stob an Fhir-bhogha and take the SW ridge to the boggy Bealach na Baintighearna. Find the lochan on the bealach which gives a good line for the steep but direct ascent to the top of Creag Mhor. A more westerly approach offers a less steep ascent but isn't so direct. Descend by the ESE ridge, the Sron nan Eun to Batavaime in Glen Lochay, then along the track to Ken Knock and the start at Badour.
Stalking Information: Ben Challum Estates. Tel: Killin 278.

Mountain: Beinn Challum, 3363 ft / 1025 m

Map: OS Sheet 50: GR 387323
Translation: Malcolm's hill

Pronunciation: cha-lam
Access Point: Kirkton Farm in Strathfillan. Leave cars by roadside
Distance: 7 miles/3000 ft; 11.2 km/914 m ascent
Approx Time: 4–6 hours
Route: From the remains of St Fillan's Chapel near the farm follow the track uphill and cross the West Highland railway line. Leave the path and take to the untracked hillside in a NE direction. Continue over grassy slopes, then over some flatter ground and a slight knoll where a fence to your right shows the direction uphill. Where the fence ends walk a few hundred metres to pass a small cairn then a short distance beyond is the south top at 3270 feet/997 m. The summit lies to the north but descend slightly west from the south top for a few metres to find the ridge which descends gradually then gives a steep pull to the large summit cairn.
Stalking Information: Loch Dochart Estate. Tel: Crianlarich 274, 275.

Mountain: Meall Glas, Sgiath Chuil, 3150 ft/960 m, 3067 ft/935 m

---

Map: OS Sheets 51: GR 431322 and GR 463318
Translation: grey-green hill, back wing
Pronunciation: myowl glas, skeea-chool
Access Point: Lubchurrin in Glen Lochay, GR 453357
Distance: 8 miles/3800 ft; 12.8 km/1158 m ascent
Approx Time: 4–7 hours
Route: Follow the stream south of Lubchurrin cottage. Keep east of the stream and follow the broad heather ridge which leads to Meall a'Churain. Follow the obvious level ridge to the summit of Sgiath Chuil. Return almost to Meall a'Churain, and descend the steep, stony slopes west half a mile to the bealach. Continue west up gradual slopes to the summit of Beinn Cheataich. Follow the ridge SW to a small cairned top then continue along a broad slightly curved ridge around the rim of Coire Cheathaich. A gentle rise leads to the summit of Meall Glas. Descend the NW ridge to Glen Lochay or take a direct line across Coire Cheathaich back to Lubchurrin.
Stalking Information: Auchlyne Estate. Tel: Killin 487.

8 THE BRIDGE OF ORCHY HILLS

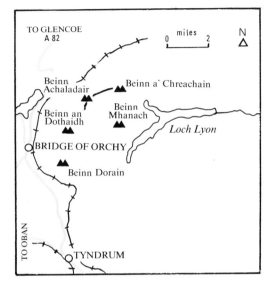

Suggested Base:	Bridge of Orchy or Tyndrum
Accommodation:	Hotels, guest houses, b/b at Bridge of Orchy, Inveroran, Kingshouse and Tyndrum, Crianlarich, Glen Coe. Youth Hostels at Crianlarich and Glencoe. Private bunkhouses at Bridge of Orchy and Kingshouse. Camping/caravan site at Glencoe. Caravan site at Tyndrum.
Public Transport:	Rail: Bridge of Orchy is on the West Highland Line. London and Glasow to Fort William. Buses: Glasgow to Fort William for Bridge of Orchy.

Mountain: Beinn Dorain, Beinn an Dothaidh,
3530 ft/1076 m, 3287 ft/1002 m

Map: OS Sheet 50: GR 326378, GR 332408
Translation: hill of the otter or small stream, hill of
the scorching
Pronunciation: doa-ran, daw-ee
Access Point: Bridge of Orchy Station, GR 301394
Distance: 8 miles/3600 ft; 12.8 km/1097 m ascent
Approx Time: 5-7 hours
Route: Leave the railway station and make for the
obvious col on the skyline between the two hills. At
the col climb due south following an obvious path up
an easy angled ridge then along the edge of a rocky
escarpment. Continue up broad grassy slopes to a
bouldery summit. The real summit lies about
656 feet/200 metres further south. Return to the col
and climb a diagonal line NNE to the summit of
Beinn an Dothaidh. The highest top is the central
one. Return to the col and descend Coire an Dothaidh
to Bridge of Orchy.
Stalking Information: Auch Estate. Tel: Oban 3014.

Mountain: Beinn Mhanach, 3130 ft/954 m

Map: OS Sheet 50
Translation: monk hill
Pronunciation: vanach
Access Point: A82 near Auch, GR 317353
Distance: 12 miles/2800 ft; 19.2 km/853 m ascent
Approx Time: 5-8 hours
Route: Leave cars by the A82. Walk down the road
past Auch, under the viaduct and up the Auch Glen
track. Continue on the track, which crosses the burn
several times to the watershed where the long steep
grassy slopes lead to Beinn a'Chuirn,
3020 feet/920 m. A broad and flat ridge runs east to
the summit of Beinn Mhanach.
Stalking Information: Auch Estate. Tel: Oban 3014.

Mountain: Beinn Achaladair, Beinn a'Chreachain, 3409 ft/1039 m, 3547 ft/1081 m

Map: OS Sheet 50: GR 345434, GR 373441
Translation: field of hard water, hill of the clamshell
Pronunciation: achalatur, chrechan
Access Point: Achallader Farm car park
Distance: 9 miles/3900 ft; 14.4 km/1189 m ascent
Approx Time: 6–8 hours
Route: From the farm head south along a track, over the railway and up Coire Achaladair. Climb to the col at the head of the corrie then turn north along the grassy ridge to the south top of Beinn Achaladair. Continue along the ridge to the summit. Descend east along the corrie rim and descend to the col at 2625 feet/800 m. Follow the broad ridge over the flat top of Meall Buidhe and then up the stony slopes of Beinn Chreachain. Descend by the steep NE ridge and once the crags are avoided turn WNW to descend grassy slopes, past the Lochan a'Chreachain, past scattered birches and through the pines of Crannach Wood. Cross the railway by a footbridge and take the track by the Water of Tulla back to the farm.
Stalking Information: Black Mount Estate. Tel: Tyndrum 225.

9 THE CRUACHAN HILLS

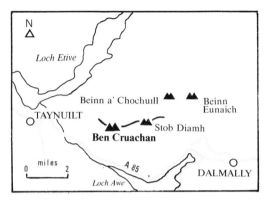

Suggested Base:	Dalmally
Accommodation:	Hotels, guest houses, b/b at Dalmally, Lochawe, Connel and Oban. Youth Hostel at Oban. Camping/caravan site at Ledaig, North Connel.
Public Transport:	Rail: Glasgow to Oban stopping at Dalmally, Taynuilt and Connel. Buses: Glasgow and Edinburgh to Oban for Dalmally, Taynuilt and Connel.

Mountain: Ben Cruachan, Stob Diamh, 3694 ft/1126 m, 3274 ft/998 m

Map: OS Sheet 50: GR 069304, GR 095308
Translation: stacky hill, peak of the stag
Pronunciation: kroo-achan, stop dyv
Access Point: Falls of Cruachan, GR 078268
Distance: 9 miles/4900 ft; 14.4 km/1494 m ascent
Approx Time: 5–8 hours
Route: Climb steeply up the path beside the Allt Cruachan to the Cruachan dam access road. For an

east–west round of Cruachan's tops follow the
reservoir's eastern shore before climbing the grassy
slopes to Stob Garbh. Continue north, descend
slightly then climb to the summit of Stob Diamh.
Follow the west ridge over the Drochaid Glas, (which
lies slightly north of the main line of the ridge) then
along a narrower bouldery crest to the main summit
of Cruachan. The ridge continues to a bealach and
the 'Taynuilt Peak', Stob Dearg. Return to the
bealach, re-ascend the main peak for some distance to
avoid the slabby face of Coire a'Bhachaill, then head
due south to Meall Cuanail and the grassy slopes back
to the Cruachan dam.
Stalking Information: Castles Estate. Dalmally 216, 347.

Mountain: Beinn a'Chocuill, Beinn Eunaich,
3215 ft/980 m, 3245 ft/989 m

Map: OS Sheet 50: GR 110328, GR 136328
Translation: hill of the hood, fowling hill
Pronunciation: cho-chil, ayneech
Access Point: Drishaig, GR 133283
Distance: 8 miles/3900 ft; 12.8 km/1189 m ascent
Approx Time: 5–8 hours
Route: From the bridge over the Allt Mhoille on the
B8077 road follow the track which runs to the head of
Glen Noe. At the 381 metres contour another short
track bears right. Follow this and continue up the SE
rib of Beinn a'Chocuill to the summit ridge and the
cairn half a mile further west. Return along the ridge
to its east end where it drops to a high bealach which
is crossed to the shoulder of Beinn Eunaich. Broad
grassy slopes lead back to the start over the subsidiary
top of Stob Maol.
Stalking Information: Castles Estate. Dalmally 216, 347.

10 GLEN ETIVE AND GLEN COE

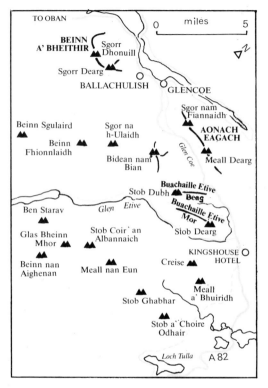

***Suggested Base*:**	Glencoe or Kingshouse
***Accommodation*:**	Hotels, guest houses and b/b in Glencoe, Ballachulish and Kingshouse. Youth hostel in Glencoe. Camping and caravan sites in Glencoe and Onich. Private bunkhouses at Clachaig and Leacantium, Glencoe and at Kingshouse Hotel.

Public Transport: Rail: Glasgow to Fort William.
Nearest station at Fort William
or Bridge or Orchy for
connecting buses. Buses:
Glasgow to Fort William for
Kingshouse, Glencoe and
Ballachulish. Oban to Fort
William for Ballachulish.

The Blackmount

Mountain: Ben Starav, Glas Bheinn Mhor and Beinn
nan Aighenan, 3537 1ft/1078 m, 3271 ft/997 m and
3150 ft/960 m

Map: OS Sheet 50: GR 126427, GR 153429 and
GR 149405

Translation: unknown, big green/grey hill and hill of
the hinds

Pronounciation: sta-rav, glas vyn voar, ben yan
Yanan

Access Point: Glen Etive, GR 136467

Distance: 12 miles/5600 ft; 19.2km/1707 m ascent

Approx Time: 5-8 hours

Route: Approach from Glen Etive where a track
crosses the river to Coileitir Farm. Follow a moorland
path, rough in places to a bridge on the Allt Mheuran
and a path on its west bank. After quarter of a mile
take the broad lower slopes of the N ridge of Ben

Starav. Follow this ridge, which narrows noticeably
and becomes quite rocky, to the triangulation pillar
near the summit. The summit cairn sits a short
distance to the south-east. From the cairn follow the
ridge SE and east to the top of Stob Coire Dheirg and
then follow another twist in the ridge to where it turns
ESE and drops to an obvious bealach west of the
grassy slopes of Glas Bheinn Mhor. From this
bealach head SSE to the broad ridge leading to Beinn
nan Aighenan. From the summit, retrace your steps
back to the bealach west of Glas Bheinn Mhor, turn
east and cross the grassy subsidiary top and finish up a
rockier ridge to the summit. Return to Glen Etive by
Glas Bheinn Mhor's east ridge, then north into the
corrie at the head of the Allt Mheuran. Glas Bheinn
Mhor's north ridge is steep and can often pose
hazards in snow or when the grass is very wet.
Stalking Information: Glen Kinglass Estate.
Tel: Tyndrum 271.

Mountain: Stob Coir'an Albannaich and Meall nan
Eun 3425 ft/1044 m, 3045 ft/928 m

Map: OS Sheet 50: GR 169433, GR 192449
Translation: peak of the corrie of the Scotsmen, hill
of the birds
Pronunciation: stop kor an alapaneech, myowl nan ayn
Access Point: As for Ben Starav
Distance: 9 miles/4300 ft; 14.4 km/1311 m ascent
Approx Time: 5–8 hours
Route: Leave Glen Etive but before reaching Coileitir
Farm head SE uphill through open woodland. Reach
the broad NW shoulder of Stob Coir'an Albannaich
and follow this ridge to the summit. The continuation
to Meall nan Eun involves an awkward switchback
ridge and crosses the subsidiary summit of Meall
Tarsuinn. The route is obvious in clear conditions but
requires careful navigation in poor ones. From the
summit of Meall nan Eun go NW across the plateau
and descend in a NW direction towards the waters of
the Allt Ceitlein. There is eventually a path on its
north bank which takes you back to Glen Etive.
Stalking Information: Glen Kinglass Estate.
Tel: Tyndrum 271.

Mountain: Stob Ghabhar and Stob a'Choire Odhair,
3566 ft/1087 m, 3094 ft/943 m

Map: OS Sheet 50: GR 230455, GR 258461
Translation: peak of the goat, peak of the dun-coloured corrie
Pronunciation: stop gowar, stop a corrie oor
Access Point: Victoria Bridge, GR 271423
Distance: 12 miles/4550 ft; 19.2 km/1387 m ascent
Approx Time: 5–8 hours
Route: From Victoria Bridge follow the track which leads west along the north bank of the Linne nam Beathach. Reach a small corrugated iron hut after about 600 metres and take the path which runs north from it beside the Allt Toaig. At GR 252446, the path crosses another burn and west of it a broad ridge lifts up to Beinn Toaig and the broad plateau-like ridge which is crowned by the summit of Stob a'Choire Odhair. Descend west to a wide knolly bealach, continue west uphill for a few hundred yards, then turn SW and up steep slopes to reach a ridge called the Aonach Eagach. Follow this ridge, which is narrow and exposed in places, to where it meets the broad SE ridge of Stob Ghabhar. Follow this to the summit. Return by way of the SE ridge.
Stalking Information: Black Mount Estate. Tel: Tyndrum 225.

Mountain: Creise and Meall a'Bhuiridh,
3609 ft/1100 m, and 3635 ft/1108 m

Map: OS Sheet 41: GR 238507, GR 251503
Translation: unknown, hill of the rutting stags
Pronunciation: kraysh, myowl a vooree
Access Point: Blackrock Cottage, GR 268531
Distance: 8 miles/3200 ft; 12.8 km/975 m ascent
Approx Time: 4–6 hours
Route: Cross the heather moorland to the mouth of the Cam Ghleann to gain the rocky slopes of Sron na Creise. Contour west to avoid rocky difficulties and ascend steep grass and scree slopes to Stob a'Ghlais Choire, the start of the main ridge which eventually terminates at Stob Ghabhar in the south. Follow the corrie rim round to a curved crest which rises to

Clachlet

Creise. Follow the ridge towards the flat top of Mam
Coire Easain. An interesting stony rib offers a way of
escape from the ridge towards a bealach at the foot of
Meall a' Bhuiridh. Take care in poor conditions as
navigation can be tricky and cornices can pose
problems in winter. Climb to the summit of Meall a'
Bhuiridh and then descend back to Blackrock
Cottage by way of the ski paraphernalia.
Stalking Information: Black Mount Estate.
Tel: Tyndrum 225.

Mountain: Beinn Sgulaird, 3074 ft/937 m

Map: OS Sheet 50: GR 053461
Translation: unknown
Pronunciation: skoolard
Access Point: Elleric, GR 035489
Distance: 4 miles/3050 ft; 6.4 km/930 m ascent
Approx Time: 3–5 hours
Route: Leave the small car park at Elleric and take
the track past the house to a bridge on the River Ure
near Glenure House. Beyond the house take the
steeply rising ground SSE as the most direct ascent to
the summit ridge. Descend either by the SW and west
ridges to the head of Loch Creran, or alternatively
NE and east to the headwaters of the River Ure, then
following the river back to Glenure.
Stalking Information: Glenure Estate. Tel: Appin 269.

Mountain: Beinn Fhionnlaidh, 3146 ft/959 m

Map: OS Sheet 41: GR 095498
Translation: Finlay's Hill
Pronounciation: byn yoonly
Access Point: Elleric, GR 035489
Distance: 9 miles/3140 ft; 14.4km/957 m ascent
Approx Time: 5–7 hours
Route: Start at Glenure, (see access for Beinn
Sgulaird), and take the lower grassy slopes in a NE
direction towards Leac Bharainn. Above this the
obvious west ridge rises gradually to the summit of
Beinn Fhionnlaidh. Descend the same way. An ascent
from Glen Etive, once the popular route to the
summit, cannot now be recommended because of
Forestry Commission activities.
Stalking Information: Glenure Estate.
Tel: Appin 269.

Mountain: Sgor na h-Ulaidh, 3261 ft/994 m

Map: OS Sheet 41: GR 111518
Translation: peak of the treasure
Pronunciation: skor na hoolya
Access Point: Achnacon, GR 118565
Distance: 8 miles/3600 ft; 12.8 km/109 m ascent
Approx Time: 4–6 hours
Route: Follow the landrover track which follows the
west bank of the Allt na Muidhe. Not far before the
cottage of Gleann-leac-na-muidhe leave the track and
take to the steep prow of Aonach Dubh a'Ghlinne, a
fierce ascent which threads through several rocky
outcrops. Continue south on the ridge to the top of
Stob an Fhuarain. Descend SW to the bealach and
follow the remains of an ancient wall and fence along
the crest of the ridge up increasingly rocky ground to
the summit. From the summit continue west to the
spur of Corr na Beinne and carefully descend its steep
north slopes to a col. From here easy slopes to the NE
take you to the headwaters of the Allt na Muidhe.
Stalking Information: National Trust for Scotland.
Tel: Ballachulish 311.

Mountain: Buachaille Etive Mor, Stob Dearg,
3353 ft/1022 m

Map: OS Sheet 41: GR 223543
Translation: big herdsman of Etive, red peak
Pronunciation: booachil etiv moar
Access Point: Altnafeath, GR 221563
Distance: 5 miles/2600 ft; 8 km/792 m ascent
Approx Time: 3–5 hours
Route: Follow the track to the bridge over the River
Coupall and pass the white climbers' hut called
Lagangarbh. Take the right fork in the path and
continue into Coire na Tulaich following the path on
the west bank of the obvious burn. Follow the path
up the corrie to its head where scree slopes offer
difficult access to a flat bealach. Turn east and cross
red and pink boulders and scree trending east then
NE along a ridge which narrows appreciably towards
the summit. The complete traverse of the Buachaille
Etive Mor ridge is a rewarding walk, from Stob Dearg
to Stob na Broige, returning to Altnafeath by the
Lairig Gartain pass to the NNW.
Stalking Information: National Trust for Scotland.
No restrictions.

Mountain: Buachaille Etive Beag, Stob Dubh,
3143 ft/958 m

Map: OS Sheet 41: GR 179535
Translation: small herdsman of Etive, black peak.
Pronunciation: booachil etiv baik
Access Point: A82 road, GR 188563
Distance: 5 miles/2400 ft; 8 km/732 m ascent
Approx Time: 3–5 hours
Route: Follow the signpost which indicates the right
of way from 'Lairig Eilde to Glen Etive'.
Take the path for about quarter of a mile before leaving
it for the open hillside in a southerly direction. Head for
the bealach to the NE of Stob Coire Raineach, and
then climb this top. Follow the obvious ridge onwards
to Stob Dubh at the end of the Buachaille Etive Beag
ridge. An alternative route climbs Stob Dubh from
Dalness in Glen Etive and takes the hill's SSW ridge.
Stalking Information: National Trust for Scotland.

Bidean nam Bian range from the Aonach Eagach Ridge

Mountain: Bidean nam Bian, 3773 ft/1150 m

Map: OS Sheet 41: GR 143542
Translation: peak of the mountains
Pronunciation: beetyan nam beeoan
Access Point: Achnambeithach, west of Loch Achtriochtan
Distance: 5 miles/3250 ft; 8 km/991 m ascent
Approx Time: 4–7 hours
Route: Follow the path which climbs up into Coire nam Beith on the west side of the stream. Pass some very fine waterfalls and climb high into the corrie. At a confluence of streams just above the 500 m contour take a SSW direction up steep slopes of grass and scree to reach the main ridge of the mountain just WNW of Stob Coire nam Beith. Follow the obvious path on the ridge to the summit, then SE to the west peak of Bidean nam Bian and then east to the summit. As an alternative descent route follow the ridge SE and return to the A82 by the Coire Gabhail or Lairig Eilde. Another alternative is to link Stob Coire nan Lochan and then descend Coire nan Lochan to the A82.
Stalking Information: National Trust for Scotland. No restrictions.

On the Aonach Eagach Ridge

Mountain: Aonach Eagach Ridge, Meall Dearg
3127 ft/953 m, Sgor nam Fiannaidh, 3173 ft/967 m

Map: OS Sheet 41: GR 161584, GR 141583
Translation: notched ridge, red hill, peak of the fair
haired warriors.
Pronunciation: myowl d-yerrack, sgor nam feeanee
Access Point: Allt-na-reigh, GR 176566
Distance: 4 miles/3000 ft; 6.4 km/914 m ascent
Approx Time: 3–5 hours
Route: Follow the path behind the house of Allt-na-
reigh up the grassy slopes of Am Bodach. There are a
few rocky outcrops but these can be avoided on the
east. To reach the crest of the Aonach Eagach ridge
follow the edge of the crags to the left of Am
Bodach's cairn in a WNW direction. A sudden drop
with 23 metre scramble on good but polished holds
starts the ridge traverse proper. Follow the crest of
the ridge to the grassy hump of Meall Dearg. From
Meall Dearg follow the line of fence posts along the
crest and then traverse the Crazy Pinnacles. This
involves some exposed scrambling on the most
sensational section of the ridge. After the Pinnacles
more fence posts accompany you on the long pull to
Stob Coire Leith, before the ridge levels out towards

the second Munro, Sgor nam Fiannaidh. It is advised
to descend due south of this summit, picking a route
with care through rocky outcrops and grassy slopes.
The alternative descent is half a mile further west of
the summit and follows a very eroded path on the
west side of Clachaig Gully. This path has a lot of
loose stones and rock on it and there is a danger of
knocking scree into the Gully where climbers could
well be put in danger. There is also the danger of
actually falling into the gully. There have been several
fatalities at this point in recent years.
Stalking Information: National Trust For Scotland.
No restrictions.

Mountain: Beinn a'Bheithir, Sgorr Dhearg,
3360 ft/1024 m, Sgorr Dhonuill, 3284 ft/1001 m

Map: OS Sheet 41: GR 056558, GR 040555
Translation: hill of the thunderbolt, red peak,
Donald's peak
Pronunciation: ben vair, sgor d-yerrack, sgor ghawil
Access Point: A828, GR 044595
Distance: 10 miles/4000 ft; 16 km 1219 m ascent
Approx Time: 5–8 hours
Route: Leave the road about 800 metres west of the
Ballachulish Bridge on a minor road which leads you
to some houses at the foot of Gleann a'Chaolais. Cars
can be left here. Follow a Forestry Commission road
south and after a while it zig-zags up steeper ground,
passes an old quarry and comes to a cross roads. Go
straight across, round another bend, over a bridge
and cross a burn at GR 047569. A cairn by the track
indicates the path which climbs SE through the forest
and on to the open hillside above the trees. Climb
south to the obvious bealach between the two peaks
of Beinn a'Bheither, Sgorr Dhonuill on your right
and Sgorr Dhearg on your left. Both peaks are easily
reached from the bealach.
Stalking Information: No restrictions.

11 THE MAMORES

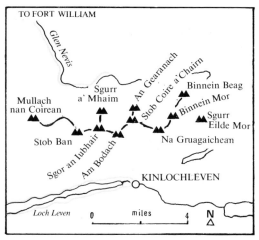

Suggested Base:	Fort William
Accommodation:	Hotels, guest houses and b/b at Fort William, Kinlochleven, Onich, Spean Bridge, Roybridge. Youth Hostel at Glen Nevis. Private Hostels at Fersit Fasgadh and Achriabach, Glen Nevis. Camping/Caravan sites at Glen Nevis, Roybridge and Spean Bridge.
Public Transport:	Rail: Glasgow to Fort William. Stations at Tulloch, Roybridge and Spean Bridge. Buses: Glasgow to Skye for Kinlochleven Fort William and Spean Bridge. Edinburgh to Skye and Fort William to Aviemore for Tulloch, Roybridge and Spean Bridge. Fort William to Glen Nevis. Fort William to Kinlochleven.

Mamore Ridge

Mountain: Binnein Beag, 3084 ft/940 m, Binnein Mor, 3701 ft/1128 m, Na Gruagaichean, 3461 ft/1055 m, Sgurr Eilde Mor, 3307 ft/1008 m

Map: OS Sheet 41: GR 222677, GR 212663, GR 203652, GR 231658
Translation: small peak, big peak, the maidens, big peak of the hind
Pronunciation: beenyan beck, beenyan mor, na grooakeechan, skoor ailta moar
Access Point: Glen Nevis Polldubh car park
Distance: 16 miles/4500 ft; 25.6 km/1372 m ascent
Approx Time: 7–10 hours
Route: Leave the car park at the head of Glen Nevis and follow the track through to Steall and along the north bank of the Water of Nevis to GR 215690. Cross the river here and climb the NE slopes of Binnein

Beag. From the summit head SSW, past a lochan and
climb the narrow and interesting NE ridge of Binnein
Mor. Continue south on a narrow ridge from the
summit to a subsidiary top and then SW to the twin
summits of Na Gruagaichean. The first summit
reached, the SE summit, is the highest. Retrace your
steps to the subsidiary top south of Binnein Mord and
continue on a narrowing ridge to the SE to Coire an
Lochain. Climb the SW slopes of Sgurr Eilde Mor
over fairly unpleasant scree and boulder fields.
Descend by NE ridge to Tom an Eite, and return to
Glen Nevis by the Water of Nevis path.
Stalking Information: British Alcan. Tel: Fort
William 2411.

Mountain: An Gearanach, 3222 ft/982 m, Stob
Choire a'Chairn, 3218 ft/981 m, Am Bodach,
3386 ft/1032 m, Sgor an Iubhair, 3286 ft/1001 m,
Sgurr a'Mhaim, 3606 ft/1099 m

Map: OS Sheet 41: GR 188670, GR 185661,
GR 176651, GR 165655, GR 165667
Translation: the complainer, peak of the corrie of the
cairn, the old man, peak of the yew, peak of the large
rounded hill
Pronunciation: an gyeranach, stob corrie a cairn, am
podach, skor an yooar, skor a vaim
Access Point: Glen Nevis Polldubh Car park
Distance: 9 miles/4000 ft; 8 km/1219 m ascent
Approx Time: 4–7 hours
Route: As route above but cross the Water of Nevis
by the wire bridge at the Steall climbing hut. Go east
past the hut, past the waterfall and a wooded buttress
until the path turns south up a small glen. Continue
on the path which eventually takes long zig-zags and
in time takes you on to the NNE spur of An
Gearanach (unmarked on the OS map). Continue
south from the summit along the short ridge to An
Garbhanach. From this top continue SW for a short
distance and climb to the summit of Stob Choire
a'Chairn. From here the obvious ridge links SW to
Am Bodach, then WNW to Sgor an Iubhair. North of
Sgor an Iubhair, the Devil's Ridge links with Stob
Choire a'Mhail. While this ridge is narrow with steep

drops on either side it poses no real problem in good conditions. From here the slopes open on to the wide quartzy summit slopes of Sgurr a'Mhaim and then a long descent northwards to Glen Nevis.
Stalking Information: British Alcan. Tel: Fort William 2411.

Mountain: Stob Ban, 3277 ft/999 m, Mullach nan Coirean, 3081 ft/939 m

Map: OS Sheet 41: GR 148654, GR 122662
Translation: light-coloured peak, summit of the corries
Pronunciation: stob baan, mullach nan kooran
Access Point: Achriabhach in Glen Nevis
Distance: 9 miles/4000 ft; 14.4 km/1219 m
Approx Time: 4–7 hours
Route: Go through the gate opposite the cottages at Achriabhach and take the footpath through the trees (not the forestry road). After a climb the footpath converges on the forestry road. Turn the next bend on the east side of the stream and out of the forest. Reach the NNE ridge of Mullach and follow this to the summit. Descend easy slopes to the SE and follow an undulating ridge which goes SE then south to the Mullach's SE top. Soon the ridge drops east to the col between the two mountains. Climb east then south up angular boulders and screes to the summit of Stob Ban. To descend take the shattered east ridge of Stob Ban to reach a stalkers' path at the head of Coire a'Mhusgain. Follow the path north down the corrie back to Achriabhach.
Stalking Information: British Alcan. Tel: Fort William 2411.

12 BEN NEVIS AND THE AONACHS

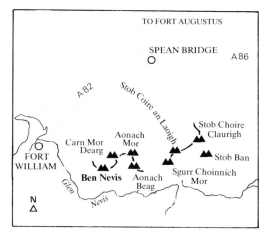

Suggested Base:	Fort William
Accommodation:	Hotels, guest houses and b/b at Fort William, Spean Bridge, Roybridge. Youth Hostels at Glen Nevis and Loch Lochy. Private Hostels at Fersit, Fasgadh and Achriabach, Glen Nevis. Camping, caravan sites at Glen Nevis, Roybridge and Spean Bridge.
Public Transport:	Rail: Glasgow to Fort William. Stations at Tulloch, Roybridge and Spean Bridge. Buses: Glasgow to Skye for Kinlochleven, Fort William and Spean Bridge. Edinburgh to Skye and Fort William to Aviemore for Tulloch, Roybridge and Spean Bridge. Fort William to Glen Nevis. Fort William to Kinlochleven.

Mountain: Ben Nevis, 4409 ft/1344 m, Carn Mor
Dearg, 4012 ft/1223 m

Map: OS Sheet 41: GR 166713, GR 177722
Translation: possibly venomous mountain, big red
hill.
Pronunciation: Nevis, Carn more jerrack.
Access Point: Achintee
Distance: 13 miles/5800 ft; 20.8 km/1769 m ascent
Approx Time: 7–10 hours
Route: Leave Achintee and follow the obvious Ben
Nevis track as far as Lochan Meall at t-Suidhe. The
track to Ben Nevis continues on a series of broad zig-
zags above but to reach Carn Mor Dearg continue
past the loch around the flanks of Carn Dearg to drop
down into the valley of the Allt a' Mhuilinn. Cross
the river near point GR 154739 and climb east up
rough bouldery slopes to Carn Beag Dearg. Continue
SSE on ridge over Carn Dearg Meadhonach to Carn
Mor Dearg. To continue to Ben Nevis follow the ridge
south and cross the Carn Mor Dearg Arete. Where
the arête abuts on to the bulk of Ben Nevis, climb
west over blocks and boulders to the summit. Take
care in this area in conditions of snow cover. Many
walkers have slipped from this point into Coire Leis
below.
Stalking Information: British Aluminium Company.
Tel: Fort William 2411.

Mountain: Aonach Beag, 4048 ft/1234 m, Aonach
Mor, 4006 ft/1221 m

Map: OS Sheet 41: GR 196715, GR 193730
Translation: little ridge, big (broad) ridge
Pronunciation: oenach bayk, oenach more
Access Point: Polldubh car park, Glen Nevis.
GR 167691
Distance: 14 miles/4880 ft; 22.4 km/1488 m ascent
Approx Time: 7–10 hours
Route: Take the footpath which runs through the
Nevis Gorge to Steall. Pass the wire bridge and
continue to the bridge and ruin by the Allt Coire
Giubhsachan. Follow the stream north to the obvious

bealach east of Carn More Dearg. Climb a steep slope
east to the bealach between Aonach Mor and Aonach
Beag. From the bealach continue north for one
kilometre over a broad and featureless ridge to the
summit of Aonach Mor. Return the way you came to
the bealach below Aonach Beag and climb rocky
slopes SE to the summit. Descend to the Allt Coire
Giubhsachan by the SW ridge and return to Steall.
Stalking Information: British Aluminium Company.
Tel: Fort William 2411.

Mountain: Sgurr Choinnich Mor, 3592 ft/1095 m,
Stob Coire an Laoigh, 3658 ft/1115 m, Stob Choire
Claurigh, 3861 ft/1177 m, Stob Ban, 3205 ft/977 m

Map: OS Sheet 41: GR 227714, GR 240725,
GR 262739, GR 266724
Translation: big peak of the moss, peak of the corrie
of the calf, peak of the corrie of clamouring, light
coloured peak
Pronunciation: skoor choanyeech more, stop corrie
an looee, stop corrie clowree, stop baan
Access Point: Coirechoille, GR 252807
Distance: 20 miles/6600 ft; 32 km/2012 m ascent
Approx Time: 10-12 hours
Route: Take the Land Rover track past Coirechoille
farm and through the forest to the Lairig Leacach.
Follow the track to the hut beside the Allt a'Chuil
Choirean. Just beyond this strike uphill in a SW
direction up the ENE ridge of Stob Ban. Follow this
ridge to the summit. Take care on the descent to the
bealach between Stob Ban and Stob Coire Claurigh as
the north slopes are precipitous and very loose.
Descend slightly to the west. Above the bealach, and
its small lochan, there is a sharp pull up to Claurigh
on loose scree and blocks. From the summit follow
the broad crest west to Stob a'Choire Leith and Stob
Coire Cath na Sine, where the ridge narrows
considerably, over Caisteal to Stob Coire an Laoigh.
The next top on the ridge is Stob Coire Easain, the
north ridge of which takes you back to Coirechoille,
but first continue on the Grey Corries ridge to Sgurr
Choinnich Mor. Unfortunately there is a big drop in
height and you have to retrace your steps back to Stob

Coire Easain, thereby doubling the ascent. Follow the north ridge of Stob Coire Easain over Beinn na Sachaich and back to Coirechoille.
Stalking Information: British Aluminium Company. Tel: Fort William 2411.

Mountain: Stob a'Choire Mheadhoin,
3629 ft/1106m, Stob Coire Easain, 3661 ft/1116 m

Map: OS Sheet 41: GR 316736, GR 308730
Translation: Peak of the middle corrie, peak of the corrie of the little waterfall
Pronunciation: stop corrie vane, stop kor esan
Access Point: Fersit, GR 350782
Distance: 9 miles/3300 ft; 14.4 km/1006 m ascent
Approx Time: 4–6 hours
Route: From Fersit follow the track to the dam at the north end of Loch Treig below the slopes of Meall Cian Dearg. Climb steep heather slopes in a SW direction to the 762 metres contour and the open ridge. After two small rises in the ridge continue SSW to the stony summit of Stob a'Choire Mheadhoin. Descend SW down rocky slopes to the bealach and ascend a rocky ridge WSW to Stob Coire Easain. From the summit follow the NW ridge and drop to the open moors of Coire Laire where a footpath takes you back to the British Aluminium Company railway line and a pleasant track back to Fersit.
Stalking Information: British Aluminium Company. Tel: Fort William 2411.

13 LOCH TREIG AND LOCH OSSIAN

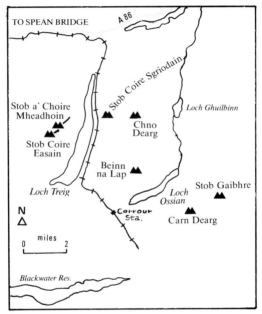

TO SPEAN BRIDGE

A 86

Stob Coire Sgriodain

Stob a' Choire
Mheadhoin

Loch Ghuilbinn

Stob Coire
Easain

Chno
Dearg

Beinn
na Lap

Loch Treig

Stob Gaibhre

Loch
Ossian

N
△

Corrour
Sta.

Carn Dearg

miles
0   2

Blackwater Res.

Suggested Base:	Fersit
Accommodation:	Private hostel at Fersit. Hotels, guest houses, b/b at Spean bridge and Roybridge.
Public Transport:	Rail: West Highland Line Glasgow to Fort William stopping at Corrour, Tulloch and Roybridge. Buses: Fort William to Aviemore stopping at Tulloch.

Mountain: Stob Coire Sgriodain, 3202 ft/976 ft, Chno Dearg, 3435 ft/1047 ft

Map: OS Sheet 41: GR 356744, GR 377741
Translation: peak of the scree corrie, red nut or red hill
Pronunciation: stop kora sgreeadan, knaw jerrack
Access Point: Fersit, GR 350782
Distance: 8 miles/3000 ft; 12.8 km/914 m ascent
Approx Time: 3–5 hours
Route: From Fersit follow a forestry road east for about 500 metres then take rough ground to the south. Climb open slopes then a craggier ridge to Sron na Garbh-bheinne. Ridge now narrows and rises to summit of Stob Coire Sgriodain. Descend south to bealach and then SE to south top of Sgriodain. Cross bumps and knolls in a ESE direction, over a double top and down to another bealach with scattered lochans. Climb easily to the crest of Meall Garbh. Follow ridge NE to the big hump of Chno Dearg. Descend easily NNW to the Strath Ossian to Fersit track.
Stalking Information: Forestry Commission. Enquire at Fersit.

Mountain: Beinn na Lap, 3074 ft/937 m

Map: OS Sheet 41: GR 376676
Translation: possibly mottled hill
Pronunciation: ben na lap
Access Point: Corrour Halt on the West Highland Railway.
Distance: 5 miles/1750 ft; 8 km/533 m ascent
Approx Time: 2–4 hours
Route: Take the train to Corrour Halt on the West Highland Line. Unless you are staying in the vicinity you will have to time your climb to suit the train timetables so check on your return train time. Follow the track east from the station to Loch Ossian. Take the left fork of the track where it splits at the loch and follow it along the north shore of the loch. Leave the track and climb north on easy angled slopes. Reach a broad ridge and follow it ENE to the summit.
Stalking Information: Forestry Commission. Enquire at Fersit.

Mountain: Sgor Gaibhre, 3133 ft/955 m, Carn Dearg, 3087 ft/941 m

Map: OS Sheets 41 and 42: GR 444674, GR 418661
Translation: goat's peak, red hill
Pronunciation: skor gyra, carn jerrack
Access Point: Corrour Halt
Distance: 12 miles/3000 ft; 19.2km/914 m ascent
Approx Time: 6–9 hours
Route: Go ENE from the station along the south shore of Loch Ossian to the cottages at the end of the loch. Avoid the forest on the south side of the loch by crossing the bridge over the outflow of the loch near Corrour Lodge and taking the path NE beside the Uisge Labhair for a short distance. Once clear of the trees cross the open hillside south to gain the slopes of Meall Nathrach Mor. Descend slightly then climb to Sgor Choinnich. Descend south to an obvious bealach and climb the broad but steeper ridge to Sgor Gaibhre. Turn WSW, descend easy slopes to broad bealach called the Mam Ban. Continue in the same direction to Carn Dearg. Descend WNW to the 'Road to the Isles' path and Corrour Station.
Stalking Information: Forestry Commission. Enquire at Fersit.

14 LOCH ERICHT TO LOCH LAGGAN

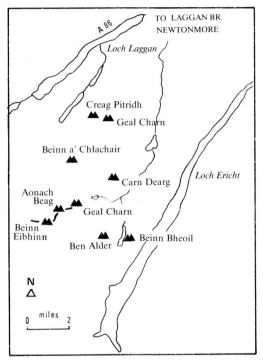

Suggested Base:	Laggan
Accommodation:	Hotels, b/b at Laggan. Hotels, guest houses and b/b at Dalwhinnie, Newtonmore. Youth Hostel at Loch Ossian. Caravan Site at Glen Truim near Newtonmore. Camping/caravan site at Newtonmore.

Public Transport:	London, Glasgow and Edinburgh to Inverness. Stations at Pitlochry, Dalwhinnie and Newtonmore. Post Buses: Newtonmore to Kinloch Laggan for Laggan.

Mountain: Carn Dearg, 3392 ft/1034 m, Geal Charn, 3714 ft/1132 m, Aonach Beag, 3655 ft/1114 m, Beinn Eibhinn, 3609 ft/1100 m

Map: OS Sheets 41 and 42: GR 504764, GR 471745, GR 458742, GR 449733

Translation: red hill, white hill, small ridge, delightful hill

Pronunciation: Carn jerrack, gyal chaarn, oenach byek, ben ayveen

Access Point: Culra Bothy, GR 355664

Distance: 14 miles/4500 ft; 22.4 km/1372 m ascent

Approx Time: 6–10 hours

Route: These are remote mountains and using Culra Bothy, ten miles (16 km) from Dalwhinnie, as an access point is the best of many choices. Phone George Oswald, gamekeeper at Dalwhinnie 224 for permission to drive from Dalwhinnie to Loch Pattack, a short distance from Culra.

From Culra Bothy climb west and NW on the southern flanks of Carn Dearg to the summit. Another cairn, slightly south, leads to the ridge which drops to a flat bealach and then rises to Diollaid a'Chairn. Beyond here the ridge narrows and leads to a steep and terraced buttress-like slope which fronts the plateau of Geal Charn. Pick a route through the terraces to the plateau. You may experience some difficulty locating the summit cairn, even in clear weather. Beyond the cairn a long slope leads WSW to a grassy bealach. Descend to the bealach and climb a short sharp rise to Aonach Beag. At the cairn, turn sharply SW to descend down rough terraces to a narrow bealach above Lochan a'Charra Mhoir. The ascent of Beinn Eibhinn involves a steep pull to the curve of a broad ridge, which in turn rises to the

cairn. To return to Culra descend south and east to
the Bealach Dubh path and follow it through the
Bealach back to the bothy.
Stalking Information: Ben Alder Estate. Tel:
Dalwhinnie 224.

Ben Alder

***

Mountain: Ben Alder, 3766 ft/1148 m, Beinn Bheoil,
3343 ft/1019 m

Map: OS Sheet 42: GR 496718, GR 517717
Translation: hill of the rock water, hill of the mouth
Pronunciation: ben awlder, ben vyawl
Access Point: Ben Alder Cottage, GR 499680. Walk
in to Ben Alder Cottage from Rannoch Mill
(GR 506576) is 8 miles (12.8 km)
Distance: 8 miles/3500 ft; 12.8 km/1067 m ascent
Approx Time: 4–6 hours
Route: Follow the path on the east bank of the stream
behind the cottage to the Bealach Breabag. Just short
of the summit of the bealach climb the broken and
craggy slopes west to a ridge high above the Garbh
Coire of Ben Alder. After half a mile cross the
expansive plateau to a high level lochan and the
summit cairn. Return to the Bealach Breabag and

climb the short and easy slope to Sron Coire na h-Iolaire. This is a short spur with cairns at either end. To the north of the west cairn a ridge drops to a stony bealach which then rises to the slabby summit slopes of Beinn Bheoil.
Stalking Information: Ben Alder Estate. Tel: Dalwhinnie 244.

Mountain: Beinn a'Chlachair, 3569 ft/1088 m, Geal Charn, 3442 ft/1049 m, Creag Pitridh, 3031 ft/924 m

Map: OS Sheet 42: GR 471781, GR 504812, GR 488814
Translation: stonemason's hill, white hill, possibly Petrie's hill
Pronunciation: ben a clachar, geel harn, craig peetrie
Access Point: Luiblea, GR 432830
Distance: 15 miles/4000 ft; 24 km/1219 m ascent
Approx Time: 7–9 hours
Route: Leave the A86 Laggan to Spean Bridge road at the concrete bridge and follow the bulldozed road up the east side of the Amhainn Ghuilbinn for about one kilometre. Turn left and follow another track for 500 metres, then right along another track which carries you around the lower slopes of Binnein Shuas to the head of Lochan na h-Earba. From the SW corner of the loch take a stalkers' path which runs up the hillside beside the Allt Coire Pitridh. After a distance of about 1.5 km bear south on open hillside towards the NE flank of Beinn a'Chlachair. Follow the slopes to an obvious shoulder and a rocky ridge around the corrie rim to the summit. Return ENE along a broad ridge which stops above a large crag. Descend north to a stalkers' path with another path a few metres lower. Follow this second path on to the west flank of Geal Charn. Go east and climb easy slopes to the flat summit. Return to the bealach west of Geal Charn and climb the easy slopes to Craig Pitridh. From the summit descend SW to regain the stalkers' path alongside the Allt Coire Pitridh.
Stalking Information: Ardverikie Estate.
Tel: Kinloch Laggan 200.

15 THE DRUMOCHTER HILLS

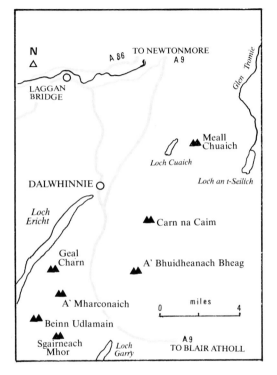

Suggested Base:	Blair Atholl
Accommodation:	Hotels, guest houses, b/b. Youth hostels at Kingussie and Pitlochry. Camping/caravan sites at Blair Atholl and Glen Truim, Newtonmore.
Public Transport:	Rail: Glasgow and Edinburgh to Inverness. Stops Pitlochry, Blair Atholl, Dalwhinnie and Kingussie. Buses: London,

Glasgow and Edinburgh to Perth
and Inverness for Blair Atholl,
Dalwhinnie, Newtonmore and
Kingussie.

Mountain: Geal-charn, 3008 ft/917 m,
A'Mharconaich, 3199 ft/975 m, Beinn Udlamain,
3314 ft/1010 m, Sgairneach Mhor, 3251 ft/991 m

Map: OS Sheet 42: GR 597783, GR 604764,
GR 579740, GR 599732
Translation: white hill, the horse place, gloomy
mountain, big stony hillside.
Pronunciation: gyal chaarn, a varkaneech, ben
ootlaman, skaarnyatch vore
Access Point: Balsporran Cottages, GR 628792
Distance: 15 miles/3750 ft; 24 km/1143 m ascent
Approx Time: 6–10 hours
Route: From the cottages cross the railway and take
the track which runs up Coire Fhar for a short
distance before taking to the open hillside of the NE
ridge of Geal-charn. Pass the three cairns higher up
the ridge at 2750 feet/838 metres then continue 800
metres west to the summit. Continue south on a
broad whalebacked ridge to a height of 3174 feet,
where a ridge appears to run off NE. The summit of
A'Mharconaich lies 800 metres along this ridge.
Return to the 3174 feet point from the summit cross a
wide bealach to the SW and continue SW on a broad
ridge to an unnamed top at 3213 feet, then over a
broad featureless plateau to the summit of Beinn
Udlamain. To reach Sgairneach Mhor descend south
to a boggy bealach. On the far side take an easterly
bearing to locate the summit cairn on the most
westerly top of the hill. From the summit descend to
Coire Dhomhain via the easterly spur, then follow the
track to the railway and the A9 about 4 km south of
Balsporran.
Stalking Information: North Drumochter Estate.
Tel: Dalwhinnie 209.

Mountain: Meall Chuaich, 3120 ft/951 m

Map: OS Sheet 42: GR 716879
Translation: Hill of the quaich
Pronunciation: myowl chooeech
Access Point: Cuaich, GR 654876
Distance: 7 miles/2000 ft; 11.2 km/610 m ascent
Approx Time: 3–5 hours
Route: Leave the A9 just south of the Cuaich cottages and follow a private road through a locked gate. In a short distance reach a track beside an aqueduct and follow it to the Loch Cuaich dam. The hill is then climbed on open heather slopes to the summit.
Stalking Information: Cuaich Estate. Tel: Dalwhinnie 254.

Mountain: Carn na Caim, 3087 ft/941 m,
A'Bhuidheanach Bheag, 3071 ft/936 m

Map: OS Sheet 42: GR 677822, GR 661776
Translation: cairn of the curve, the little yellow place
Prononiciation: caarn a kym, a vooanach vek
Access Point: Balsporran Cottages
Distance: 8 miles/2000 ft; 12.8 km/610 m ascent
Approx Time: 4–6 hours
Route: Leave the A9 just south of Balsporran and climb steep heathery slopes raked with shallow gullies to Meall a'Chaoruinn. Continue east and follow a fence to the summit of A'Bhuidheanach Bheag. North of the summit the fence crosses an area of peat at the head of Coire Chuirn. Follow the fence to Carn a Caim, two rounded tops on either side of a shallow depression. Follow open and obvious slopes SW back to the A9 in Drumochter Pass.
Stalking Information: South Drumochter Estate. Tel: Dalwhinnie 209.

16 THE TARF AND TILT HILLS

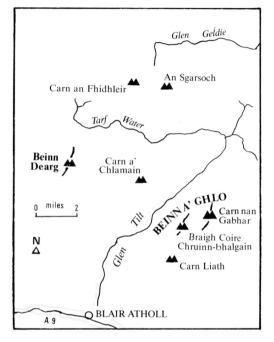

Suggested Base:	Blair Atholl. Braemar for An Sgarsoch and Carn an Fhidhleir.
Accommodation:	Hotels, guest houses, b/b. Youth hostels at Pitlochry and Braemar. Camping/caravan sites at Blair Atholl and Braemar.
Public Transport:	Rail: Glasgow and Edinburgh to Inverness. Stops Blair Atholl. Glasgow and Edinburgh and Inverness to Aberdeen. Ongoing bus services to Braemar. Buses: Glasgow and Edinburgh to Inverness. Stop at Blair Atholl.

Glasgow and Edinburgh and
Inverness to Aberdeen.
Aberdeen to Braemar.

Mountain: Beinn a' Ghlo: Carn Liath, 3199 ft/975 m,
Braigh Coire Chruinn-bhalgain, 3510 ft/1070 m, Carn
nan Gabhar, 3704 ft/1129 m

Map: OS Sheet 43: GR 936698, GR 946724, GR 971733
Translation: grey hill, upland of the corrie of round
blisters, hill of the goats.
Pronunciation: kaarn leea, bray corrie kroon
valakan, kaarn nan gower
Access Point: Marble Lodge, GR 898717
Distance: 12 miles/4000 ft; 19.2 km/1219 m ascent
Approx Time: 6–8 hours
Route: Permission is given (on small payment) by
Atholl Estate at the factor's Office at Old Blair to
drive up Glen Tilt as far as Marble Lodge. Behind
Balaneasie Cottage on the south bank of the River Tilt
climb grassy slopes to the headwaters of the Fender
Burn. Traverse the hillside SE, past the pines beside
Craig-choinnich Lodge and then east up steep heather-
covered slopes to the summit of Carn Liath. Follow
a twisting ridge north. This soon broadens out as it
approaches Braigh Coire Chruinn-bhalgain. Continue
NE along the ridge for one kilometre before dropping
down grassy slopes to cross the Bealach na Fhiodha.
Continue east to the slopes which lead to another
bealach between Airgiod Bheinn and Carnnan Gabhar
and finally NE along a broad and easy ridge to the twin
cairns of Carn nan Gabhar. Descend back to Glen Tilt by
the north ridge to the bridge below Allt Fheannach.
Stalking Information: Tel: Blair Atholl 355.

Mountain: Beinn Dearg, 3307 ft/1008 m

Map: OS Sheet 43: GR 853778
Translation: Red Hill
Pronunciation: Ben Jerrack
Access Point: Old Blair, GR 867667
Distance: 15 miles/2750 ft; 24 km/838 m ascent
Approx Time: 6–8 hours

Route: From Old Blair walk up the private road in
Glen Banvie and continue up east side of the Allt an t-
Seapail to a bothy beside the Allt Sheicheachan. A
track continues along the NW side of this stream to
the 800 m contour. From there follow the broad and
easy ridge north to the summit.
Stalking Information: Tel: Blair Atholl 355.

Mountain: Carn a'Chlamain, 3159 ft/963 m

Map: OS Sheet 43: GR 916758
Translation: hill of the kite or buzzard
Pronunciation: kaarn a klaavan
Access Point: Glen Tilt, GR 908720
Distance: 6 miles/2400 ft; 9.6 km/732 m ascent
Approx Time: 3–4 hours
Route: A couple of miles south of Forest Lodge in
Glen Tilt a long ridge runs down from the summit of
Carn a'Chlamain just east of the Allt Craoinidh.
Climb steep initial slopes then follow the curving
ridge to the summit.
Stalking Information: Tel: Blair Atholl 355.

Mountain: An Sgarsoch, 3300 ft/1006 m, Carn an
Fhidhleir, 3261 ft/994 m

Map: OS Sheet 43: GR 933836, GR 905842
Translation: the place of sharp rocks, hill of the fiddler
Pronunciation: an skarsoch, kaarn an yeelar
Access Point: Linn o'Dee.
Distance: 25 miles/3000 ft; 40 km/914 m ascent
Approx Time: 10–12 hours
Route: Follow north bank of the River Dee to White
Bridge and then along the Geldie Burn to Geldie
Lodge. Follow a bulldozed track WSW to its highest
point. Continue SW over peat hags and climb the NE
slopes of Carn an Fhidhleir to reach the north ridge
close to the summit. Drop SSE along a broad ridge
and then down the east side of the ridge to reach the
bealach at 2297 ft/700 m. From there climb NE to the
flat summit of An Sgarsoch. Return to Geldie Lodge
by following the north ridge and then west of
Sgarsoch Bheag over peaty ground to reach the
bulldozed track again.
Stalking Information: Tel: Braemar 216.

17 THE CAIRNWELL HILLS

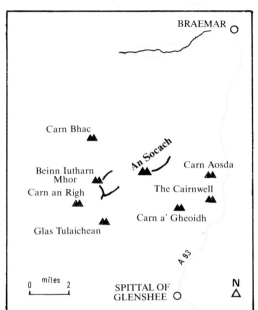

Suggested Base:	Braemar
Accommodation:	Hotels at Spittal of Glenshee, Hotels, guest houses and b/b at Braemar, Ballater and Inverey. Youth hostels at Braemar, Ballater and Muir of Inverey. Caravan site at Ballater
Public Transport:	Rail: London, Glasgow and Edinburgh to Aberdeen for onward bus services to Braemar. Buses: London, Edinburgh, Glasgow and Inverness to Aberdeen for onward bus services to Braemar.

Mountain: An Socath, 3097/944 m, Carn Bhac,
3104 ft/946 m, Beinn Iutharn Mhor, 3428 ft/1045 m,
Carn an Righ, 3376 ft/1029 ft, Glas Tulaichean,
3448 ft/1051 ft

Map: OS Sheet 43: GR 080800, GR 051832,
GR 045792, GR 028773, GR 051760
Translation: the projecting place, hill of peat hags,
big hill of the edge, hill of the king, green hills
Pronunciation: an sochkach, kaarn vachk, byn
yooarn vore, kaarn an ree, glas tooleechan
Access Point: Inverey
Distance: 26 miles/6000 ft; 41.6 km/1829 m ascent.
This includes the five mile (8 km) walk in each way
from Inverey to Altanour Lodge.
Approx Time: 10–16 hours
Route: Walk up the length of Glen Ey from Inverey to
Altanour Lodge, (ruin). Climb An Socath by way of
its NE ridge, Carn Cruinn, and return to Altanour.
Follow the course of the Allt an Odhar west and then
NW into its shallow corrie. The summit of the flat
topped Carn Bhac is only a short distance away to the
NW. From the summit follow the broad ridge SW to
the SW top and follow another broad ridge south to a
broad bealach. From here a steep climb on heather
and scree will take you to the bald summit ridge of
Beinn Iutharn Mhor. From the cairn continue south
and SW, contouring round the easy slopes of Mam
nan Carn. Reach the low col and climb the steeper
heather slopes to the summit of Carn an Righ.
Retrack to Mam nan Carn and then descend SSE to
the col at the head of Gleann Mor. An ascent of Glas
Tulaichean's north ridge leads to the summit. Return
to Altanour by the north ridge, Loch nan Eun and
descend by the Allt Beinn Iutharn to the broad valley.
Stalking Information: Mar Estate. Tel: Braemar 216.

Mountain: The Cairnwell, 3061 ft/933 m, Carn
a'Gheoidh, 3199 ft/975 m, Carn Aosda, 3008 ft/917 m

Map: OS Sheet 43: GR 135773, GR 107767, GR 134792
Translation: From Carn Bhalg, hill of bags, hill of the
goose, hill of age.

Pronunciation: cairnwell, kaarn a yowee, kaarn oesh
Access Point: Devil's Elbow, GR 140780
Distance: 5 miles/1900 ft; 8 km/579 m ascent
Approx Time: 3–5 hours
Route: Start just south of the ski area and climb
heather slopes to the summit. Descend NNW past the
top chairlift point and continue on a broad ridge with
snow fences. Just before the Cairnwell-Aosda col
turn west and drop to another col, the lowest point
between The Cairnwell and Carn a' Gheoidh.
Continue SW past Carn nan sac and west over a small
plateau to Carn a'Gheoidh. Return the way you came
to the Cairnwell-Aosda col. From there ascend NE
then east along a broad ridge to the flat summit of
Carn Aosda. Descend south by bulldozed tracks and
roads to the Cairnwell road.
Stalking information: Mar Estate. Tel: Braemar 216.

18 GLENSHEE AND LOCHNAGAR HILLS

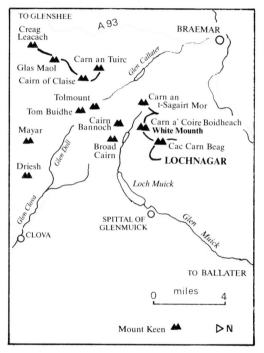

TO GLENSHEE

A 93

BRAEMAR

Creag Leacach

Carn an Tuirc

Glen Callater

Glas Maol

Cairn of Claise

Tolmount

Carn an t-Sagairt Mor

Tom Buidhe

Cairn Bannoch

Carn a' Coire Boidheach
White Mounth

Mayar

Broad Cairn

Cac Carn Beag
LOCHNAGAR

Glen Doll

Driesh

Loch Muick

Glen Clova

SPITTAL OF GLENMUICK

Glen Muick

CLOVA

TO BALLATER

0   miles   4

Mount Keen   ▷ N

Suggested Base:	Braemar or Glen Doll
Accommodation:	Hotels, guest houses and b/b in Braemar, Ballater, Glenshee, Milton of Clova. Youth Hostels at Ballater, Braemar, Glen Doll. Camping/caravan sites at Ballater.
Public Transport:	Rail: London, Glasgow and Edinburgh to Dundee and

Aberdeen. Buses: Limited bus
transport to southern glens.
Aberdeen to Braemar and
Ballater. Dundee to Kirriemuir
and Blairgowrie for onward post
bus service. Post Buses: Kirriemuir
to Glen Doll YH, Blairgowrie to
Spittal of Glenshee.

Mountain: Glas Maol, 3504 ft/1068 m, Creag
Leacach, 3238 ft/987 m

Map: OS Sheet 43: GR 166765, GR 155746
Translation: green/grey bare hill, slabby rock
Pronunciation: glas moel, krayk lyechach
Access Point: Summit of A93
Distance: 6 miles/1700 ft; 9.6 km/518 m ascent
Approx Time: 4–6 hours
Route: Leave the car park at the summit of the
Cairnwell road and climb ski slopes east to the Meall
Odhar ski tows. Keep to the right of the tow lines,
cross Meall Odhar to a flat col. Continue SW to the
great dome of Glas Maol. Head SW over schistose
mossy screes to the ridge which leads to Creag
Leacach. From the summit continue to the SW top
and then turn NW down a steep slope to the saddle
behind Meall Gorm. From the saddle descend NNE
by a grassy re-entrant to the valley below. Head
downstream, cross to the north side of the burn to a
footpath and cross the Allt a'Ghlinne Bhig by a
bridge to reach the A93 a couple of kilometres south
of your starting point.
Stalking Information: Invercauld Estate. Tel:
Braemar 267.

Mountain: Carn an Tuirc, 3343 ft/1019 m, Cairn of
Claise, 3491 ft/1064 m, Tolmount, 3143 ft/958 m,
Tom Buidhe, 3140 ft/957 m

Map: OS Sheets 43 and 44: GR 174804, GR 185789,
GR 210800, GR 214788
Translation: hill of the boar, hill of the hollow, hill of
the valley, yellow hill

Pronunciation: kaarn an toork, kaarn an claes, tolmount, tom booee
Access Point: A93 north of Cairnwell. GR 148800
Distance: 11 miles/2600 ft; 17.6 km/792 m ascent
Approx Time: 5-8 hours
Route: Cross the Cairnwell Burn by an ancient bridge and follow the Allt a'Garbh-coire east on a path for one kilometre and cross the tributary coming down from the NE. Climb due east to the summit of Carn an Tuirc. Continue east then as the slope steepens towards Coire Kander turn SE down a wide and grassy ridge. Reach a wide saddle below Cairn of Claise and continue SSE up slopes to the summit. Go ENE to a peaty col and then up wide slopes to Tolmount. Descend SW skirting the upper reaches of a shallow valley and then SE up grassy slopes to the summit of Tom Buidhe. From here walk west over Ca Whims, skirt the slopes of Cairn of Claise on its south side and follow a fence line SW to the route of the Monega Road which follows the spur of Sron na Gaoithe. Leave the ridge on its north side near its termination and follow grass slopes to the Allt a' Garbh-coire and then the bridge at the starting point.
Stalking Information: Invercauld Estate.
Tel: Braemar 267 and Balmoral Estate Ranger Tel: Ballater 55434.

Mountain: Carn an t-Sagairt Mor, 3435 ft/1047 m, Carn a' Coire Bhoidheach, 3668 ft/1118 m

---

Map: OS Sheets 43 and 44: GR 208843, GR 226845
Translation: big hill of the priest, hill of the beautiful corrie.
Pronunciation: kaarn an takarsht moar, kaarn a corrie vawyach
Access Point: Auchallater on the A93
Distance: 15 miles/2900 ft; 24 km/884 m ascent
Approx Time: 7-10 hours
Route: Leave Auchallater and follow estate road to Loch Callater Lodge. By the lodge enclosure a path strikes uphill and traverses the hillside above Loch Callater. As it gains height it zig-zags slightly before reaching a bealach below the west slopes of Carn an t-Sagairt Mor. Follow the path up the slopes until it

begins to contour to the SE. Leave the path here and
climb directly to the summit following a fence line.
From the summit continue NE, cross over Carn an t-
Sagairt Beag and reach the edge of the plateau. About
500 metres east the Stuic rises and is worth a visit.
From there walk another 500 metres over stony
tundra to Carn a'Coire Boidheach. Return by the
south side of t-Sagairt Mor and Glen Callater.
Stalking Information: Balmoral Estate Ranger.
Tel: Ballater 55434.

Mountain: Cairn Bannoch, 3320 ft/1012 m, Broad
Cairn, 3274 ft/998 m

Map: OS Sheet 44: GR 223826, GR 240815
Translation: possibly peaked hill, broad cairn
Pronunciation: kaarn bannoch, broad kaarn
Access Point: Car park in Glen Muick
Distance: 17 miles/2400 ft; 27.2 m/732 m ascent
Approx Time: 8–10 hours
Route: Leave the car park at the road end in Glen
Muick and take the bulldozed track on the NE shores
of Loch Muick. Pass through the Glas-allt-Shiel
woods and 100 metres after the woods take the right
fork in the path to follow the Allt an Dubh-loch up to
its source in the Dubh Loch itself. Follow the shore of
the loch to its NW point and follow the stream which
flows down from behind Creag an Dubh-loch.
Continue to the summit cone of Cairn Bannoch.
Continue SE over the undulating plateau to Cairn of
Gowal and then go east to a broad saddle and the
gentle climb to Broad Cairn. Continue east to reach a
rough track which soon becomes a bulldozed brack.
At a wooden shelter continue east for 300 m then bear
left down the path which leads to Loch Muick.
Follow the path along the south shore back to Spittal
of Glenmuick.
Stalking Information: Balmoral Estate Ranger. Tel:
Ballater 55434.

Mountain: Lochnagar, 3789 ft/1155 m

Map: OS Sheet 44: GR 244862
Translation: named after Lochan na Gaire in NE

Corrie. Little loch of the noisy sound
Pronunciation: loch-na-gar
Access Point: Spittal of Glenmuick car park
Distance: 12 miles/2700 ft; 19.2 km/823 m ascent
Approx Time: 5–8 hours
Route: Take the path which runs along the edge of the
plantation to cross to the other side of the glen at Allt-
na-giubhsaich. Take the path which runs along the
south bank of the burn through the pinewoods and
reach a track which is followed west for about 3 km to
the bealach which leads through to Gelder Shiel. At
this point take an obvious path WSW across a slight
hollow and then more steeply to the Foxes' Well on
the left of the path. Soon the slope steepens again
before 'The Ladder' and the top of the summit ridge.
A short descent across a wide col and another climb
leads to the flat summit ridge of the mountain. Walk
along the rim of the corrie, past Cac Carn Mor and
the deep chasm of the Black Spout to the summit cone
of Cac Carn Berag where you'll find the trig point. An
alternative descent goes via Glas Allt and steep zig-
zags to the woods of Glas-allt-Shiel. The track is then
followed back to Glen Muick.
Stalking Information: Balmoral Estate Ranger. Tel:
Ballater 55434.

Mountain: Driesh, 3107 ft/947 m, Mayar,
3045 ft/928 m

Map: OS Sheet 44: GR 271736, GR 241738
Translation: From Gaelic dris, bramble or thorn
bush, possibly from m'aighear, my delight, or from
magh, a plain.
Pronunciation: dreesh, may-yer
Access Point: Braedownie, GR 288757
Distance: 8 miles/2700 ft; 12.8 km/823 m ascent
Approx Time: 4–6 hours
Route: Start at the Forestry Commission (FC) car
park quarter of a mile past Braedownie Farm. A track
from Acharn, near the Youth Hostel in Glen Doll,
crosses the White Water to a forestry fence which
runs up the hill for just under 1000 feet/305 m. Where
the fence contours off to the west continue directly
upwards to the top of The Scorrie where the slopes

ease off. Continue to the summit. From Driesh follow the long and obvious ridge west for about 3.2 km to Mayar. To descend follow grassy slopes NNE to the edge of Corrie Fee. Continue on the SE side of the Fee Burn past small waterfalls to a path at the foot of one of the steeper sections. Follow this ENE down the lower corrie, over a stile and into the forest. The path soon becomes a forest road which eventually runs past the Youth Hostel to the FC car park.
Stalking Information: Enquiries at Youth Hostel. Tel: Clova 236.

Mountain: Mount Keen, 3081 ft/939 m

Map: OS Sheet 44: GR 409869
Translation: from monadh caoin, smooth or pleasant hill
Pronunciation: mount keen
Access Point: Glen Tanar House, GR 473957
Distance: 15 miles/2500 ft; 24 km/762 m ascent
Approx Time: 6–10 hours
Route: Start at the end of the public road which runs up Glen Tanar. Walk past a sawmill and through a gate which leads to an estate road. Follow this through pinewoods for about 4.8 km and on up the open glen, crossing the river twice. At the third crossing (GR 407896) ascend the Mounth Road south by a bulldozed track through heathery slopes. Diverge SE up the path to Mount Keen's summit.
Stalking Information: Glen Tanar Estate. Tel: Aboyne 2451.

19 NORTHERN CAIRNGORMS

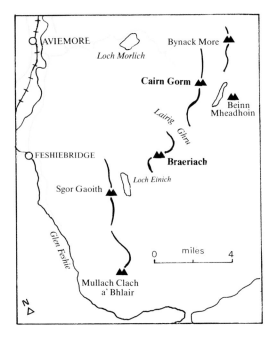

Suggested Base:	Kingussie or Aviemore
Accommodation:	Hotels, guest houses and b/b in Laggan, Newtonmore, Kingussie, Kincraig, Aviemore, Boat of Garten, Carrbridge and Nethybridge. Youth Hostels in Kingussie and Aviemore. Private hostel in Glen Feshie. Camp sites at Coylumbridge, Loch Morlich, Newtonmore. Caravan sites in Aviemore, Newtonmore, Kingussie and Boat of Garten.

Public Transport: Rail: London, Glasgow and
Edinburgh to Inverness. Stations
at Kingussie and Aviemore.
Buses: London, Glasgow and
Edinburgh via Perth to Inverness
for Kingussie and Aviemore.
Aviemore to Coire Cas
(Cairngorm ski bus operates all
year round).

Mountain: Mullach Clach a'Bhlair, 3343 ft/1019 m,
Sgor Gaoith, 3668 ft/1118 m

Map: OS Sheet 43: GR 883927, GR 903989
Translation: summit of the stone of the plain, peak of
the wind
Pronunciation: moolach clach a vaar, skor goo-ee
Access Point: Achlean in Glen Feshie
Distance: 16 miles/2700 ft; 25.6 km/823 m ascent
Approx Time: 6–8 hours
Route: Leave Achlean in Glen Feshie by the
Foxhunter's Path which climbs Carn Ban Mor
eastwards above the Allt Fhearnagan. Continue over
the shoulder south of Carn Ban Mor until the
footpath joins up with a bulldozed track. Follow this
track SW and south over the Moine Mhor and past
the head of Coire Garbhlach. Beyond this point
another track joins from the west but continue south
and where the track begins to bend due east leave it
and climb the easy stony slopes of Mullach Clach
a'Bhlair. Return to Carn Ban Mor over the bulldozed
track or wander straight across the Moine Mhor on
bearings. From Carn Ban Mor descend NNE to the
broad bealach above the Fuaran Diotach then climb
the easy slopes of Sgor Gaoith. Return to Achlean via
Carn Ban Mor.
Stalking Information: Glen Feshie Estate: Tel:
Kingussie 453.

Mountain: Braeriach, 4252 ft/1296 m

Map: OS Sheets 36 and 43: GR 953999
Translation: brindled upland

Braerich Plateau

Pronunciation: brae-reeach
Access Point: Car Park in Coire Cas of Cairngorm
Distance: 13 miles/2750 ft; 20.8 km/838 m ascent
Route: Leave the car park by the footpath to Coire an
t-Sneachda. Reach the Sneachda burn and then head
across the heathery moorland west to the obvious
notch of Chalamain Gap. Go through the gap and
descend to the Lairig Ghru and the Sinclair Hut.
Climb the hillside behind the hut by way of the
obvious footpath and reach the broad bealach.
Finally climb SW to the edge of Coire Bhrochain and
then follow the corrie lip to the summit.
Stalking Information: Rothiemurchus Estate. Tel:
Aviemore 810858.

Mountain: Cairngorm, 4085 ft/1245 m, Beinn
Mheadhoin, 3878 ft/1182 m

Map: OS Sheet 36: GR 005041, GR 024017
Translation: blue hill, middle hill
Pronunciation: Cairngorom, byn vee-an
Access Point: Coire Cas car park
Distance: 11 miles/5500 ft; 17.6 km/1676 m ascent
Approx Time: 6–10 hours
Route: Leave the car park and climb Cairngorm by
way of the Sron an Aonaich and the 'Ptarmigan

Bowl'. A dubious alternative is to climb up through the ski paraphernalia in Coire Cas by way of bulldozed tracks. From the summit of Cairngorm descend south into Coire Raibert and down the steep and loose path beside the burn to Loch Avon. Follow the path round the west head of the loch, past the Shelter Stone, and up into Coire Etchachan. From Loch Etchachan climb stony slopes NE to the granite tors of Beinn Mheadhoin. The largest of these is the summit and can be climbed by an easy scramble from its north side. Descend steep slopes, avoiding Creag Dubh, to the foot of Loch Avon. Cross the stream at its outlet from the loch and follow the footpath west to the Saddle at the head of Strath Nethy. Climb the SE slopes of Cairngorm to Ciste Mhearaid which is just below the col between Cairngorm and Cnap Coire na Spreidhe. Return to car park.
Stalking Information: No restrictions.

Mountain: Bynack More, 3576 ft/1090 m

Map: OS Sheet 36: GR 042063
Translation: big cap
Pronunciation: bie-nack moar
Access Point: Glenmore Lodge, GR 992097
Distance: 12 miles/2500 ft; 19.2 km/762 m ascent
Approx Time: 5–8 hours
Route: Leave parking area just beyond Glenmore Lodge and follow the forestry track into the Pass of Ryvoan. Continue through the Pass, past Lochan Uaine. Quarter of a mile beyond the lochan take another path east to Bynack Stable and the River Nethy. Cross the river and follow the footpath SE over the lower shoulder of Bynack More. Follow this path to its highest point then leave it to bear south up the north ridge to the summit. Return the same way or by Strath Nethy.
Stalking Information: Nature Conservancy Council. Tel: Aviemore 810287.

20 SOUTHERN CAIRNGORMS

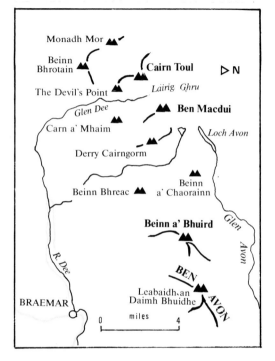

Suggested Base:	Braemar
Accommodation:	Hotels at Spittal of Glenshee, hotels, guest houses and b/b at Braemar, Ballater and Inverey. Youth Hostels at Ballater, Braemar and Inverey. Private Hostel at Braemar. Caravan/camping site at Braemar.

Public Transport: Rail: London, Glasgow and Edinburgh to Aberdeen for onward bus service to Braemar. Buses: London, Edinburgh, Glasgow and Inverness to Aberdeen for onward bus service to Braemar.

Cairn Toul

Mountain: The Devil's Point, 3294 ft/1004 m, Cairn Toul, 4242 ft/1293 m

Map: OS Sheets 36 and 43: GR 976951, GR 964972
Translation: from original name of hill Bod an Deamhain, penis of the devil, from carn an t-sabhail, hill of the barn.
Pronunciation: devil's point, kaarn towal
Access Point: Linn of Dee
Distance: 23 miles/3700 ft; 36.8 km/1128 m ascent
Approx Time: 8–12 hours
Route: Take the private road from Linn of Dee to Derry Lodge. Follow the track up Glen Luibeg to the Lairig Ghru. Follow the path which skirts the southern slopes of Carn a' Mhaim and drops to Glen Dee. Cross the river to Corrour Bothy. A worn path leads west behind the bothy up steep zig-zags above the Allt a' Choire Odhair. From the col at the head of

the corrie head south then bear east to the summit
The Devil's Point. Return to the col. Follow the
broad grassy ridge which rises north. Follow the ridge
to Stob Coire an t-Saighdeir and then to Cairn Toul.
Stalking Information: Mar Lodge Estate. Tel:
Braemar 216

Mountain: Monadh Mor, 3651 ft/1113 m, Beinn
Bhrotain, 3816 ft/1163 m

Map: OS Sheet 43: GR 938942, GR 954923
Translation: big hill, hill of the mastiff
Pronunciation: monagh moar, byn vrotan
Access Point: Linn of Dee
Distance: 23 miles/3000 ft; 36.8 km/914 m ascent
Approx Time: 8–12 hours
Route: Take the private road west from Linn of Dee
to White Bridge. Continue past the Chest of Dee and
along the path to its end. Take to the rough moor and
enter Glen Geusachan. Follow the stream up the glen
and climb to the outflow from Loch nan Stuirteag.
Turn south and climb the obvious ridge of Monadh
Mor to the summit. Head south to another top at
3642 feet/1110 m and then descend SE above the head
of Coire Cath nam Fionn. From the col continue SE
to the summit of Beinn Bhrotain. Continue SE over
Carn Cloich-mhuilinn and down its east ridge to Glen
Dee.
Stalking Information: Mar Lodge Estate. Tel:
Braemar 216

Mountain: Ben Macdui, 4295 ft/1309 m, Carn
a'Mhaim, 3402 ft/1037 ft, Derry Cairngorm,
3789 ft/1155 m

Map: OS Sheets 36 and 43: GR 988989, GR 994952,
GR 017980
Translation: hill of the black pig, cairn of the large
round hill, blue hill of Derry (from doire; a thicket)
Pronunciation: byn macdooee, kaarn a vame, derry
cairngorom
Access Point: Linn of Dee
Distance: 19 miles/4500 ft; 30.4 km/1372 m ascent
Approx Time: 8–12 hours

Ben Macdui

Route: Take the private road from Linn of Dee to
Derry Lodge. Cross the Derry Burn by the bridge west
of Derry Lodge. Follow the track to the Luibeg
Bridge and then leave the track to climb the SE ridge
of Carn a'Mhaim. The NW top is the summit. From
here follow the narrowing ridge in a NNW direction
to a wide col at 2625 feet/800 m. Climb the steep and
stony slopes due north to the summit of Beinn
Macdui. Descend east over wide bouldery and
featureless slopes to the edge of Coire Sputan Dearg
and follow the ridge NE to a col just west of Creagan
a Choire Etchachan. Skirting the SW slopes of
Creagan a Choire Etchachan descend south to the
bealach north of Derry Cairngorm. Climb bouldery
slopes south to the summit. Return to Derry Lodge by
Carn Crom.
Stalking Information: Mar Lodge Estate. Tel:
Braemar 216.

Mountain: Beinn Bhreac, 3054 ft/931 m, Beinn
a'Chaorainn, 3550 ft/1082 m

Map: OS Sheets 36 and 43: GR 058971, GR 045013
Translation: speckled hill, hill of the rowan
Pronunciation: byn vrechk, byn a choeran
Access Point: Linn of Dee
Distance: 18 miles/2700 ft; 28.8 km/823 m ascent
Approx Time: 7–10 hours

Route: Take the private road to Derry Lodge.
Continue on the bulldozed track on the east side of
Glen Derry for just over a mile then strike uphill over
heathery slopes and through trees to the col between
Meall an Lundain and Beinn Bhreac. From here
climb NNE to the summit. Continue NW then north
across the Moine Bhealaidh to Beinn a'Chaorainn.
Return to Derry Lodge by the Lairig an Laoigh track.
Stalking Information: Mar Lodge Estate. Tel:
Braemar 216.

Mountain: Ben Avon, Leabaidh an daimh Bhuidhe,
3842 ft/1171 m, Beinn a'Bhuird, 3924 ft/1196 m

Map: OS Sheets 36 and 43: GR 132019, GR 093006
Translation: bed of the yellow stag, hill of the table
Pronunciation: lyepay an dyv vooee, byn a voord
Access Point: Invercauld Bridge
Distance: 25 miles/4500 ft; 40 km/1372 m ascent
Approx Time: 11–15 hours
Route: Leave your car at Keiloch and continue on the
private road to Glen Quoich. Continue past the ruins
of Slugain Lodge to the end of the path beyond the
boulder of Clach a'Chleirich. From there climb NNE
to the obvious saddle at 3182 feet/970 m called The
Sneck. From here climb east up gravelly slopes to the
summit tor of Beinn Avon, Leabaidh an Daimh
Bhuidhe. Return to the Sneck, cross it and continue
ESE over featureless plateau to the North Top of
Beinn a'Bhuird. Return to Glen Quoich by the south
top and carn Fiaclach where a stalkers' path takes you
back to just north of Slugain Lodge.
Stalking Information: Invercauld Estate. Tel:
Braemar 224.

21 LAGGAN AND THE MONADHLIATH

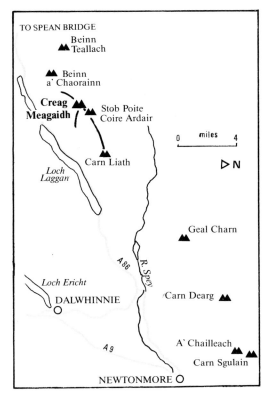

TO SPEAN BRIDGE

Beinn Teallach

Beinn a' Chaorainn

Creag Meagaidh

Stob Poite Coire Ardair

Carn Liath

Loch Laggan

0   miles   4

▷ N

Geal Charn

A 86

R. Spey

Loch Ericht

DALWHINNIE

Carn Dearg

A 9

A' Chailleach

Carn Sgulain

NEWTONMORE

Suggested Base:	Newtonmore
Accommodation:	Hotels, guest houses and b/b at Newtonmore and Laggan. Youth Hostel at Kingussie. Caravan site at Glen Truim and caravan/ camping site at Newtonmore.

Public Transport:	Rail: London, Glasgow and Edinburgh to Inverness. Station at Newtonmore. Bus to Laggan, Roybridge and Fort William. Buses: London, Glasgow and Edinburgh to Inverness. Stops at Newtonmore.

Mountain: Carn Dearg, 3100 ft/945 m, A'Chailleach, 3051 ft/930 m, Carn Sgulain, 3018 ft/920 m

Map: OS Sheet 35: GR 635024, GR 681042, GR 684059
Translation: red hill, the old woman, hill of the basket or of the old man.
Pronunciation: kaarn jerrag, a kaalyach, kaarn skoolin
Access Point: Glen Banchor, GR 693998
Distance: 15 miles/2750 ft; 241 cm/838 m ascent
Approx Time: 6–8 hours
Route: Drive up Glen Banchor to the parking area above Shepherd's Bridge. Follow the footpath north beside the Allt a'Chaorainn till it ends in a turning point. Drop down to the stream and cross by a footbridge which is hidden from the path. Climb heathery slopes NNE to the rounded summit of A'Chailleach. Descend north into a deep glen and then continue north on steep and tussocky grass to the summit of Carn Sgulain. From the summit follow a line of fence posts west then SW over undulating plateau crossing several minor tops. At Carn Ban, leave the fence posts and go south to a short and steep climb to the summit of Carn Dearg. From here continue on the narrow ridge south to a bealach and drop east into Gleann Balloch down broad heathery slopes. A narrow footpath follows the stream back into Glen Banchor from where another track beside the River Calder takes you back to Shepherd's Bridge.
Stalking Information: Banchor Mains Farm. Tel: Newtonmore 215.

Mountain: Geal Charn, 3038 ft/926 m

Map: OS Sheet 35: GR 561988
Translation: white hill
Pronunciation: gyal chaarn
Access Point: Garva Bridge
Distance: 9 miles/2000 ft; 14.4 km/610 m ascent
Approx Time: 4–6 hours
Route: From the bridge follow the path which runs up the SE side of the Feith Talagain. At the end of the path cross the Allt Coire nan Dearcag and climb the heather covered SW ridge of Geal Charn direct to the summit. Return by Beinn Sgiath and the SW ridge.
Stalking Information: Tel: Fort William 2433.

Mountain: Creag Meagaidh, 3707 ft/1130 m, Carn Liath, 3300 ft/1006 m, Stob Poite Coire Ardair, 3455 ft/1053 m

Map: OS Sheets 34 and 42: GR 418875, GR 472904, GR 429889
Translation: bogland rock, grey hill, peak of the pot of the high corrie
Pronunciation: crayk meggie, kaarn leea, stop potya kor aardar
Access Point: Aberarder Farm
Distance: 16 miles/4500 ft; 25.6 km/1372 m ascent
Approx Time: 8–12 hours
Route: Behind the Nature Conservancy Council (NCC) buildings at Aberarder Farm a good path crosses the lower moorland. After a mile or so, as the track climbs through birch trees strike uphill NNE on the heather clad slopes of Carn Liath. From the summit head NW to follow the edge of Coire Ardair over Meall an t-Snaim, Sron Garbh Choire and the east top of Stob Poite Coire Ardair. Continue west to the summit. From the cairn continue west then south as the slopes fall away to 'The Window', a deep col. Climb the steep slopes on to the plateau, past Mad Meg's Cairn to the true summit. Leave the cairn behind and walk east to the edge of the corrie and follow the ridge SE and east over Puist Coire Ardair, and Creag Mhor. Drop down open slopes to Aberarder.
Stalking Information: NCC. Tel: Aviemore 810287.

Creag Meagaidh

Mountain: Beinn Teallach, 3002 ft/915 m, Beinn a'Chaoruinn, 3451 ft/1052 m

Map: OS Sheets 34 and 41: GR 361860, GR 386851
Translation: forge hill, hill of the rowan
Pronunciation: byn tyellach, byn a choerin
Access Point: Roughburn GR 377813
Distance: 11 miles/3750 ft; 17.6 km/1143 m ascent
Approx Time: 4–7 hours
Route: Follow the forestry road NW for 800 metres to the slopes below Meall Clachaig. Follow a firebreak north to reach a deer fence and a gate near the road junction. Climb north and then bear NE up easy slopes to the south top and then along the broad ridge to the summit of Beinn a'Chaoruinn. Continue on the ridge to the north top and then drop NNW, then west to the col at the head of the Allt a'Chaoruinn. Climb the slopes west to reach the NE ridge of beinn Teallach. Follow the ridge to the summit.
Stalking Information: Fountain Forestry.
Tel: Inverness 224948.

22 LOCH LOCHY, LOCH ARKAIG AND LOCH EIL

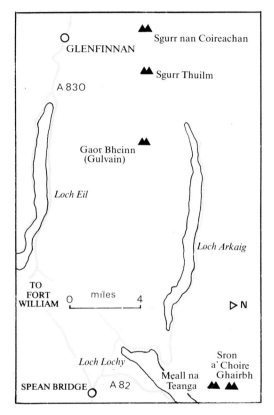

GLENFINNAN

Sgurr nan Coireachan

Sgurr Thuilm

A 830

Gaor Bheinn
(Gulvain)

Loch Eil

Loch Arkaig

TO
FORT
WILLIAM

miles

0   4

▷ N

Loch Lochy

SPEAN BRIDGE

A 82

Meall na
Teanga

Sron
a' Choire
Ghairbh

Suggested Base:	Spean Bridge
Accommodation:	Hotels, guest houses and b/b at Spean Bridge, Roybridge, Fort William, Invergarry. Youth Hostel at Fort William (Glen

| | Nevis) and Loch Lochy. Camping/Caravan sites at Spean Bridge, Roybridge and Invergarry. |
| *Public Transport:* | Rail: Glasgow to Mallaig. Stations at Spean Bridge. Buses: Oban and Fort William to Inverness for Laggan Locks and Loch Lochy. |

Mountain: Sron a' Choire Ghairbh, 3067 ft/935 m, Meall na Teanga, 3008 ft/917 m

Map: OS Sheet 34: GR 223945, GR 220924
Translation: nose of the rough corrie, hill of the tongue
Pronunciation: srawn a corrie ghirav, myowl na tyenga
Access Point: North end of Loch Lochy.
Distance: 13 miles/4250 ft; 20.8 km/1295 m ascent
Approx Time: 6–9 hours
Route: At the north end of Loch Lochy cross by the Laggan Locks to Kilfillan. Follow the Forestry Commission track SW above the loch. After about 3.2 km follow a track which climbs from the forest track uphill NW then west to the obvious pass between the two hills. From the top of the pass, climb Meall na Teanga first, return to the head of the pass then climb Sron a' Choire Ghairbh. Descend by the latter's long eastern spur directly to Kilfillan.
Stalking Information: Forestry Commission.
Tel: Fort William 2184 or Invergarry 209.

Mountain: Gulvain, 3238 ft/987 m

Map: OS Sheets 40 and 41: GR 003876
Translation: from Gaor Bheinn, possibly filthy hill
Pronunciation: Goolvan
Access Point: Drumsallie, GR 960794
Distance: 12 miles/3700 ft; 19.2 km/1128 m ascent
Approx Time: 6–8 hours
Route: Start from Drumsallie on the A830 Fort

William to Mallaig road and follow the track up the east side of the Fionn Lighe river. Continue up the glen for about 5.6 km till you reach the foot of the SSE ridge of Gulvain. Climb the ridge, past a craggy knoll and the south top and climb the narrowing ridge to the summit.
Stalking Information: Locheil Estates. Tel: Fort William 2433.

Mountain: Sgurr Thuilm, 3159 ft/963 m, Sgurr nan Coireachan, 3136 ft/956 m

---

Map: OS Sheet 40: GR 939879, GR 903880
Translation: peak of the round hillock, peak of the corries
Pronunciation: skoor hoolim, skoor nam korachan
Access Point: Glenfinnan
Distance: 12 miles/4000 ft; 19.2 km/1219 m ascent
Approx Time: 6–9 hours
Route: Follow the private road up the right side of the River Finnan below the railway viaduct. Just over 3 km up the glen pass the Corryhully bothy and continue on the track until it crosses the stream that drains Coire Thollaidh and Coire a'Bheithe. Cross the stream and head for the obvious spur that leads to Druim Coire a'Bheithe and the summit of Sgurr Thuilm. From the cairn return south for a short distance to join the main ridge which runs west over the ups and downs of Beinn Gharbh and Meall an Tarmachain to the final climb to Sgurr nan Coireachean. From the summit descend SE and then climb to Sgurr a' Choire Riabhaich where the ridge becomes very steep sided and care should be taken. Follow the ridge to the track NE of the Corryhully Bothy.
Stalking Information: Glenfinnan Estate.
Tel: Kinlocheil 270.

23 KNOYDART AND LOCH QUOICH

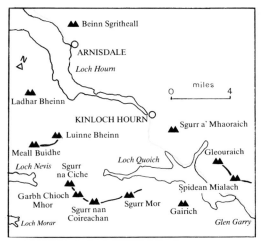

Suggested Base:	Invergarry
Accommodation:	Hotels, guest houses and b/b at Invergarry, Spean Bridge, Sheil Bridge and Tomdoun. Private hostels at Inverie and Barrisdale.
Public Transport:	Rail: Glasgow to Mallaig. Stations at Spean Bridge and Fort William for onward bus services. Mallaig for ferry to Inverie. Buses: Glasgow to Skye. Edinburgh and Perth to Skye for Invergarry. Fort William to Inverness for Invergarry. Post Buses: Invergarry to Kinloch Hourn for Loch Quoich-side. Kyle of Lochalsh to Arnisdale for ferry to Barrisdale on Knoydart. Ferries: Arnisdale to Kinloch Hourn for Barrisdale, Mallaig to Inverie on Loch Nevis.

Mountain: Sgurr na Ciche, 3415 ft/1041 m, Garbh Chioch Mhor, 3323 ft/1013 m

---

Map: OS Sheets 33 and 40: GR 902966, GR 909961
Translation: peak of the breast, big rough place of the breast
Pronunciation: skoor na keesh, garav kee-ach voar
Access Point: Strathan
Distance: 13 miles/3000 ft; 20.8 km/914 m ascent
Approx Time: 6–8 hours
Route: Follow the track from Strathan to Glen Dessarry. Take the uphill path behind the house of Upper Glendessarry to reach the Allt Coire nan Uth and climb diagonally uphill to reach the saddle of Bealach nan Gall. Climb west up increasingly rocky slopes to the ridge which leads to Garbh Chioch Bheag and then Garbh Choich Mhor. Beyond the summit the ridge narrows considerably on the descent to Feadan na Ciche. From the pass take the obvious grassy ramp which leads to a succession of grassy ledges which lead through the rocky screes and blocks to the summit rib. From the summit return to the Feadan Gap. From here descend SW down the course of the Allt Coire Ciche, steep in places to a grassy terrace from which easy slopes drop down to the Mam na Cloich' Airde pass. Follow the path back to Glen Dessarry and Strathan.
Stalking Information: Tel: Perth 28151.

Mountain: Sgurr nan Coireachan, 3127 ft/953 m, Sgurr Mor, 3290 ft/1003 m

---

Map: OS Sheets 33 and 40: GR 933958, GR 965980
Translation: peak of the corries, big peak
Pronunciation: skoor nan korachan, skoor mor
Access Point: Strathan
Distance: 14 miles/5000 ft; 22.4 km/1524 m ascent
Approx Time: 9–10 hours
Route: Take the Glen Dessarry track to where it crosses the Allt Coire nan Uth. Climb the mountain's southern slopes directly to a cairned top. The main summit is a little to the north. An ancient fence bounds the head of Coire nan Uth and this should be followed. The ridge continues to An Eag and then NE

along another ridge which drops to a bealach and then climbs Sgurr Beag. Beyond another small dip in the ridge a 600 feet/183 m climb takes you to the summit of Sgurr Mor. *Stalking Information*: Tel: Perth 28151.

Mountain: Gairich, 3015 ft/919 m

Map: OS Sheet 33: GR 025995
Translation: roaring
Pronunciation: gaareech
Access Point: Loch Quoich dam
Distance: 9 miles/2500 ft; 14.4 km/762 m ascent
Approx Time: 4–6 hours
Route: From the south end of the dam a path leads to an old stalkers' path which runs south over boggy moorland to the edge of a forestry plantation. Here, another path runs due west, up the Druim na Geld Salaich. Once the broad ridge crest is reached the path peters out. The going is easy however, and the broad ridge should be followed west to the final steep pull to Gairich. At the foot of this final rise a path re-appears, but after a while it runs out on to the south face. Don't be tempted by it but continue climbing on the crest of the ridge to the spacious summit and large cairn.
Stalking Information: Tel: Fort William 2433.

Mountain: Luinne Bheinn, 3080 ft/939 m, Meall Buidhe, 3104 ft/946 m

---

Map: OS Sheets 33 and 40: GR 868008, GR 849990
Translation: hill or anger, or hill of melody, yellow hill
Pronunciation: loonya vyn, myowl booee
Access Point: Barrisdale
Distance: 12 miles/4500 ft; 19.2 km/1372 m ascent
Approx Time: 6–9 hours
Route: Take the Inverie path to the head of Mam Barrisdale. Above the pass, the NW ridge of Luinne Bheinn drops down in a sharp even line. Follow this ridge to the summit. At the east end of Luinne Bheinn a steep southern flank drops to a broad knolly ridge which eventually forms Druim Leac a' Shith. This ridge borders a remote and desolate north corrie of Meall Buidhe. Follow this ridge, over its complex bumps and knolls, and climb gradually to the more

obviously defined NE ridge of Meall Buidhe which takes you to to the east summit. The true summit is a few hundred yards to the west.
Stalking Information: Tel: Blair Atholl 240.

Mountain: Ladhar Bheinn, 3346 ft/1020 m

Map: OS Sheet 33: GR 824040
Translation: hoof or claw hill
Pronunciation: laarven
Access Point: Barrisdale
Distance: 9 miles/3500 ft; 14.4 km / 1067 m ascent
Approx Time: 4–6 hours
Route: A bridge crosses the river above Barrisdale to a path which in turn crosses the saltings to meet a stalkers' path below Creag Bheithe. Follow this path up zig-zags, round the nose of Creag Bheithe and through some woodland into Coire Dhorrcail. Cross the Allt Coire Dhorrcail and climb grassy slopes west to the ridge of Druim a' Choire Odhair. Follow this narrowing ridge to the crest of Stob a' Choire Odhiar, then on to the summit ridge of Ladhar Bheinn. A cairn at this point is often mistaken for the summit, but the true summit lies a few hundred yards to the west. To complicate matters further an OS trig point lies at the western end of the ridge at a height of 3313 feet. The best descent lies SE, over the ridges above Coire Dhorrcail and Coire na Cabaig, over Aonach Sgoilte and down the east ridge to Mam Barrisdale.
Stalking Information: Tel: Blair Atholl 240.

Mountain: Beinn Sgritheall, 3195 ft/974 m

Map: OS Sheet 33: GR 836126
Translation: hill of screes
Pronunciation: byn skreehal
Access Point: Opposite Eilean Rarsaidh on the Arnisdale road, GR 815120
Distance: 6 miles/3200 ft; 9.6 km/975 m ascent
Approx Time: 4–6 hours
Route: Follow the old hill track to Glenelg up through some scattered woods and make for an obvious break in the rocky escarpment above you. Above the crags turn right and cross some moorland

with scattered lochans. The west ridge of Sgritheall is now quite obvious and leads to the summit. Continue east on the ridge which soon narrows again. Follow it to the Bealach Arnisdale; a stream offers the best guide back to Arnisdale itself and the Loch Hourn road.
Stalking Information: Tel: Glenelg 312 and 244.

Mountain: Sgurr a'Mhaoraich, 3369 ft/1027 m

Map: OS Sheet 33: GR 984065
Translation: peak of the shellfish
Pronunciation: skoor a vooreach
Access Point: Quoich Bridge, GR 014040
Distance: 7 miles/3200 ft; 11.2 km/975 m ascent
Approx Time: 4–6 hours
Route: Follow a stalkers' path which starts just SW of the bridge. Follow the path north up the ridge of Bac nan Canaichean to Sgurr Coire nan Eireallach and then across a slight dip to its NW top. From here another ridge leads west to the summit of Sgurr a'Mhaoraich.
Stalking Information: Tel: Blair Atholl 240.

Mountain: Gleouraich, 3396 ft/1035 m, Spidean Mialach, 3268 ft/996 m

Map: OS Sheet 33: GR 039054, GR 066043
Translation: uproar or noise, peak of wild animals
Pronunciation: glyawreech, speetyan meealach
Access Point: Loch Quoich, GR 029030
Distance: 7 miles/3600 ft; 11.2 m/1097 m ascent
Approx Time: 4–6 hours
Route: A cairn on the west side of the Allt Coire Peitireach indicates the beginning of what becomes a very good stalkers' path. Above the 304.8 metres contour the path moves on to a grassy spur and then zig-zags uphill and continues all the way to the rocky crest of the hill. A wide stony ridge continues east, drops and then rises to Craig Coire Fiar Bhealeach. Beyond another stalkers' path zig-zags down to the Fiar Bhealach and then another climb brings you to the summit of Spidean Mialach. Descend easy slopes to the SW, passing Loch Fearna and down the slopes of Coire Mheil to the roadside.
Stalking Information: Tel: Blair Atholl 240.

24 GLEN SHIEL HILLS

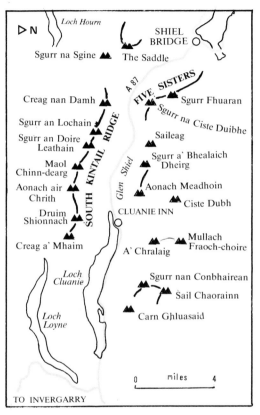

Suggested Base:	Shiel Bridge
Accommodation:	Hotels, guest houses and b/b at Shiel Bridge, Dornie, Cluanie and Glenelg. Youth Hostel at Ratagan.

Public Transport: Train: Inverness to Kyle of
Lochalsh. Onward bus services.
Buses: Kyle of Lochalsh and
Plockton to Shiel Bridge and
Letterfearn. Glasgow and Fort
William to Skye. Edinburgh and
Perth to Skye. Inverness to Skye.
All stopping at Shiel Bridge. Post
Buses: Kyle of Lochalsh to
Arnisdale for Shiel Bridge.

Mountain: The Saddle, 3314 ft/1010 m, Sgurr na
Sgine, 3100 ft/945 m

Map: OS Sheet 33: GR 936131, GR 946113
Translation: the saddle, peak of the knife
Pronunciation: the saddle, skoor na skeena
Access Point: Achnagart, GR 968142
Distance: 10 miles/4700 ft; 16 km/1433 m ascent
Approx Time: 5–7 hours
Route: Start SE of the quarry at Achnagart. A
stalkers' path leads west to a bealach between Biod an
Fhithich and Meallan Odhar. From here go south
then SW to the bottom of the Saddle's east ridge,
known as the Forcan Ridge. Follow this ridge, knife
edged and exposed in places to Sgurr na Forcan.
Continue west down a steep rock pitch with good
holds and traverse a narrow ridge to the east top of
the Saddle and then the summit. The OS trig point is
further on and lower than the cairn which marks the
summit. Descend to the Bealach Coire Mhalagain
down rough bouldery slopes and climb to the NW top
of Sgurr na Sgine. Follow a rocky ridge SE to the
summit cairn. Descend by way of Faochag and its fine
NE ridge.
Stalking Information: Glen Shiel (Cluanie) Estate.
Tel: Glenshiel 282.

Mountain: The South Glen Shiel Ridge: Creag a'Mhaim, 3107 ft/947 m, Druim Shionnach, 3238 ft/987 m, Aonach air Chrith, 3350 ft/1021 m, Maol Chinn-dearg, 3218 ft/981 m, Sgurr an Doire Leathain, 3314 ft/1010 m, Sgurr an Lochain, 3294 ft/1004 m, Creag nan Damh, 3012 ft/918 m

Map: OS Sheet 33: GR 088078, GR 074085, GR 051083, GR 032088, GR 015099, GR 005104, GR 983112
Translation: rock of the large round hill, ridge of the fox, trembling hill, bald red hill, peak of the broad thicket, peak of the little loch, rock of the stags
Pronunciation: crayk a vaim, drim heeanach, oenach ayr chree, moel chan dyerack, skoor an dira lehan, skoor an lochan, creag nam dav
Access Point: Cluanie Inn
Distance: 15 miles/6000 ft; 24 km/1829 m ascent
Approx Time: 7–11 hours
Route: Take the old road from Cluanie Inn to Glen Loyne and climb Creag a'Mhaim by the streams which flow down Coirean an Eich Bhric. Follow the broad ridge NW to Druim Shionnach, descend a short dip then a gradual rise brings you to Aonach air Chrith. This is the high point of the ridge. Continue now on the narrowest section of the ridge towards Maol Chinn-dearg. On the north spur of this hill a stalkers' path runs into Coire Chuil Droma Bhig, offering a convenient exit for those who would rather split the ridge into two days walking. Continue NW to the minor top of Sgurr Coire na Feinne, then west to the flat topped Sgurr an Doire Leathain. From here the ridge dips again, before rising to Sgurr an Lochain. Another minor top follows, Sgurr Beag, although this top can be contoured on its south side to reach the col before the last Munro of the ridge, Creag nan Damh. From here a fence leads west to the Bealach Duibh Leac and a stalkers' path to Glen Shiel.
Stalking Information: Glen Shiel (Cluanie) Estate. Tel: Glenshiel 282.

Five Sisters' Ridge

Mountain: Five Sisters of Kintail: Sgurr na Ciste
Duibhe, 3369/1027 m, Sgurr Fhuaran, 3504 ft/1068 m

Map: OS Sheet 33: GR 984149, GR 978167
Translation: peak of the black chest, meaning
obscure
Pronunciation: skoor na keesta ghoo, skoor ooaran
Access Point: Glenshiel Bridge
Distance: 10 miles/5000 ft; 16 km/1524 m ascent
Approx Time: 6–8 hours
Route: From Glenshiel Bridge climb the steep and
unrelenting slopes of Sgurr na Ciste Duibhe. Make
for the ridge west of Sgurr nan Spainteach. From here
follow the narrow ridge west to Sgurr na Ciste
Duibhe's summit. Avoiding a false ridge which runs
north of the peak continue NW and descend to the
Bealach na Craoibhe. Turn north and climb over
Sgurr na Carnach to a V-shaped gap of the Bealach na
Carnach. From here a short and steep ascent leads to
the summit of Sgurr Fhuaran. A descent can be made
from here by the east ridge to Glenlicht House but
most walkers continue north for the full traverse,
over Sgurr nan Saighead and down the NW spur to
Sgurr an t-Searraich from where steep rough slopes
lead to the cottages at Shiel Bridge.
Stalking Information: National Trust for Scotland.
Tel: Glenshiel 219.

Mountain: Saileag, 3146 ft/959 m, Sgurr a' Bhealaich Dheirg, 3405 ft/1038 m, Aonach Meadhoin, 3291 ft/1003 m, Ciste Dhubh, 3222 ft/982 m

---

Map: OS Sheet 33: GR 017148, GR 035143, GR 049137, GR 062166
Translation: little heel, peak of the red pass, middle hill, black chest
Pronunciation: saalak, skoor a vyaleech yerak, oenach vain, keesta doo
Access Point: Glenlicht House
Distance: 11 miles/5500 ft; 17.6 km/1676 m ascent
Approx Time: 6–8 hours. Walk in to Glenlicht House from Croe Bridge is four miles (6.4 km)
Route: From Glenicht House climb SE up the grassy wall of Meall a' Charra, then up the long grassy spur which leads to Saileag. Follow the ridge east above the Fraoch-choire where a sweeping rise takes you to Sgurr a'Bhealaich Dheirg. The summit cairn lies about 50 metres north of the main ridge. Return to the ridge and continue ESE to Aonach Meadhoin and a short narrow section of ridge to another top on Sgurr an Fhuarail. A wide ridge now runs north and dips to a green bealach. Above this pass a steep and narrow ridge runs north to Ciste Dhubh from where the NW ridge can be descended to the Allt Cam-ban. This can be difficult to cross in times of spate.
Stalking Information: National Trust for Scotland. Tel: Glenshiel 219.

Mountain: A' Chralaig, 3674 ft/1120 m, Mullach Fraoch-choire, 3615 ft/1102 m

---

Map: OS Sheet 33 and 34: GR 094148, GR 095171
Translation: basket or creel, heather-corrie peak
Pronunciation: a chraalik, moolach froech-chora
Access Point: West end of Loch Cluanie
Distance: 8 miles/3500 ft; 12.8 km/1067 m ascent
Approx Time: 5–8 hours
Route: Leave the A87 near the west end of Loch Cluanie where a stalkers' track leaves the road to run through the An Caorrann Mor to Glen Affric. Don't follow the track but climb steeply NE up grassy slopes on A'Chralaig. Continue until the angle eases on the

south ridge, and follow this ridge to the large summit cairn. Continue north along a grassy ridge and cross the top of Stob Coire na Cralaig. After this the ridge narrows considerably and several pinnacles have to be crossed before reaching the summit of Mullach. Either return to the start the way you came, or alternatively drop down into Coire Odhar (steep at first) and return by the track in An Caorrann Mor.
Stalking Information: Ceannacroc Estate.
Tel: Dalchreichart 40243.

Mountain: Carn Ghluasaid, 3140 ft/957 m, Sgurr nan Conbhairean, 3642 ft/1110 m, Sail Chaorainn, 3287 ft/1002 m

Map: OS Sheet 34: GR 146125, GR 130139, GR 134155
Translation: hill of movement, peak of the keeper of the hounds, hill (heel) of the rowan
Pronunciation: kaarn ghlooasat, skoor nan konavaran, sale choeran
Access Point: Lundie, Loch Cluanie
Distance: 10 miles/3500 ft; 16 km/1067 m ascent
Approx Time: 6–8 hours
Route: Leave the A87 at Lundie, about 2.5 miles (4 km) west of Cluanie dam. Follow the old military road west for a few hundred metres then follow the obvious and well constructed stalkers' path which climbs the south slopes of Carn Ghluasaid all the way on to its extensive plateau. Cross the plateau to the summit which sits fairly close to the edge of the north face. Continue west then NW along the broad ridge, crossing Creag a' Chaorainn then west to cross a col and the final climb to Sgurr nan Conbhairean. From here descend north down an easy ridge to a col and climb Sail Chaorainn by its easy angled SSW ridge. To return follow the ridge back towards Conbhairean but bypass the summit on its west side. Continue SW to a col above Gorm Lochan and continue a short distance to Drochaid an Tuill Easaich. (A Top unnamed on the 1:50000 map). Descend the south ridge back to the old military road which will take you back to Lundie.
Stalking Information: Ceannacroc Estate.
Tel: Dalchreichart 40243.

25 GLEN AFFRIC AND STRATHFARRAR

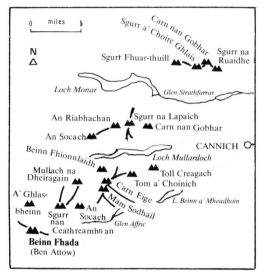

Suggested Base:	Shiel Bridge or Cannich
Accommodation:	Hotels, guest houses and b/b in Shiel Bridge, Dornie, Kyle of Lochalsh, Cannich, Tomich. Youth Hostels at Ratagan, Cannich and Alltbeith. Camping/caravan sites at Beauly, Muir of Ord and Drumnadrochit
Public Transport:	Train: Inverness to Wick and Thurso, and Inverness to Kyle of Lochalsh. Station at Muir of Ord for onward post bus service. Buses: Inverness to Dingwall, Tain and Dornoch. Inverness to

Garve and Ullapool for Beauly
and Muir of Ord for onward post
bus service. Post Buses: Beauly
to Tomich for Struy and
Cannich. Muir of Ord to Strathconon for Inverchoran.

Mountain: A' Ghlas-bheinn, 3012 ft/918 m

Map: OS Sheet 33: GR 008231
Translation: greenish-grey hill
Pronunciation: a' glasvin
Access Point: Strath Croe, GR 977222
Distance: 8 miles/3000 ft; 12.8 km/914 m ascent
Approx Time: 4–6 hours
Route: Leave the car park near Dorusduain and take
the path which climbs to the Bealach na Sroine. Just
beyond the top of the bealach climb south on the
slopes of Meall Dubh, steeply at first and then easing
off considerably. Continue SSW over a knobbly ridge
to the summit. To descend continue south down easy,
then steeper slopes to the Bealach an Sgairne and a
delightful stalkers' path which carries you all the way
back to the start.
Stalking Information: Tel: Killilan 262.

Mountain: Beinn Fhada (Ben Attow), 3386 ft/1032 m

Map: OS Sheet 33: GR 018192
Translation: long hill
Pronunciation: byn ata
Access Point: Strath Croe
Distance: 11 miles/3750 ft; 17.6 km/1143 m ascent
Approx Time: 6–8 hours
Route: From the car park near Dorusduain take the
stalkers' path which runs up to the Bealach an Sgairne.
After crossing the stream which flows down from
Coire an Sgairne take another path which runs up into
the corrie and climb the slopes of Meall a'Bhealaich.
Follow this ridge south to where it abuts on to the
great summit plateau of Beinn Fhada known as the
Plaide Mor. Continue SE along the edge of the
plateau to the summit cairn.
Stalking Information: NTS Tel: Glenshiel 219.

Mountain: An Socach, 3018 ft/920 m, Sgurr nan Ceathreamhnan, 3776 ft/1151 m, Mullach na Dheiragain, 3222 ft/982 m

Map: OS Sheets 25 and 33: GR 088230, GR 057228, GR 081259
Translation: the snout, peak of the quarters, possibly summit of the hawk
Pronunciation: an sochkach, skoor nan keroanan, moollach na yerakan
Access Point: Alltbeithe, GR 080202
Distance: 16 miles/5500 ft; 25.6 km/1676 m ascent
Approx Time: 7–12 hours
Route: Reach the Alltbeithe from either Loch Beinn a'Mheadhoin in Glen Affric (10 miles/16 km) or a shorter route through the An Caorrann Mor from Cluanie. From Alltbeithe a footpath beside the Allt na Faing leads directly to the ridge just west of An Socach. Go east to the summit. Return to the ridge and follow it west again. Climb grassy terraces to the top of Stob Coire nan Dearcag. Continue on the gently rising ridge to the east top of Ceathreamhnan. Continue over rocky ground to the summit. Rough ground to the NE of the summit leads to a descent to a sharp rib above An Gorm-lochan. The ridge now broadens and offers an easy walk along the length of Creag a'Choir' Aird to Mullach na Dheiragain. Return to Ceathreamhnan and descend to Alltbeithe by the south ridge of the west top.
Stalking Information: National Trust for Scotland. Tel: Glenshiel 219.

Mountain: Toll Creagach, 3458 ft/1054 m, Tom a'Choinich, 3645 ft/1111 m, Carn Eige (Eighe), 3881 ft/1183 m, Beinn Fhionnlaidh, 3297 ft/1005 m, Mam Sodhail (Mam Soul), 3871 ft/1180 m

Map: OS Sheet 25: GR 194283, GR 163273, GR 123262, GR 115282, GR 120253
Translation: rocky hollow, hill of the moss, file hill, Finlay's hill, hill of the barns
Pronunciation: tow kraykach, towm a choanyeech, kaarn aya, byn yoony, mam sool
Access Point: Glen Affric, GR 215242

Distance: 23 miles/7600 ft; 36.8 km/2316 m ascent
Approx Time: 10–16 hours
Route: From the car park near the head of Loch
Affric a path runs north into Gleann nam Fiadh. As it
turns west into the glen another path leaves the
riverside and climbs NW over the Bealach Toll Easa.
Toll Creagach can easily be climbed from the summit
of this pass, and so can Tom a' Choinich. From here
continue west over the undulating, and in places
rough, ridge. Cross the deep notch of the Garbh-
bhealach and continue past the needles of Stob Coire
Dhomhnuill (easily turned on the left), round the
head of Coire Dhomhain to Creag na h-Eige and then
to the great dome of Carn Eige itself. From the
summit head north to Beinn Fhionnlaidh, a long pull
involves a 1000 ft/305 m drop and a pull up the other
side. Return towards Carn Eige but the climb back to
the summit can be avoided by a traverse up the west
slopes between Carn Eige and Mam Sodhail.
Continue to the summit cairn, a massive structure built
round the OS pillar. Return to Glen Affric via the ridge
which runs SE over Mullach Cadha Rainich and Sgurr
na Lapaich avoiding the latter's craggy eastern cliffs.
Stalking Information: Tel: Cannich 351.

Mountain: Carn nan Gobhar, 3255 ft/992 m, Sgurr
na Lapaich, 3772 ft/1150 m, An Riabhachan,
3704 ft/1129 m, An Socach, 3507 ft/1069 m

Map: OS Sheet 25: GR 182344, GR 161351,
GR 134345, GR 100333
Translation: hill of the goats, peak of the bog, the
brindled, greyish one, the snout
Pronunciation: kaarn nan gower, skoor na lahpeech,
an reeavachan, an sochach
Access Point: Mullardoch Dam
Distance: 19 miles/6200 ft; 30.4 km/1890 m ascent
Approx Time: 9–13 hours
Route: Follow the stalkers' path up the east bank of
the Allt Mullardoch and into Coire an t-Sith.
Continue to climb north up the steep slopes of Creag
Dhubh where the ridge is reached. Follow the ridge
WSW to the summit of Carn nan Gobhar. Follow the
broad ridge NW over a wide grassy saddle beyond

which a steeper rib leads to the summit of Sgurr na Lapaich. Leave the summit by the SW shoulder and descend steeply to a col, the Bealach Toll an Lochain. Follow the rim of An Riabhachan's NE corrie to the NE top and then across to the summit itself. From the summit cross to the SW top and here the main ridge turns NW towards the west top where a twist in the ridge leads down to another bealach below An Socach. Climb easily to the broad summit. To return to Glen Cannich follow the south ridge which then sweeps round to the SE and the long indistinct path alongside Loch Mullardoch. *Stalking Information*: Balmore and Cozac Estate Keeper. Tel: Cannich 339.

Mountain: Sgurr Fhuar-thuill, 3441 ft/1049 m, Sgurr a'Choire Ghlais, 3553 ft/1083 m, Carn nan Ghobhar, 3255 ft/992 m, Sgurr na Ruaidhe, 3258 ft/993 m

---

Map: OS Sheet 25: GR 235437, GR 259430, GR 273439, GR 289426
Translation: peak of the cold hollow, peak of the greenish-grey corrie, hill of the goats, peak of redness
Pronunciation: skoor ooar hil, skoor a chora ghlash, kaarn nan gower, skoor na rooy
Access Point: Braulen Lodge, GR 237387
Distance: 14 miles/5000 ft; 22.4 km/1524 m ascent
Approx Time: 6–10 hours
Route: Access to Glen Strathfarrar is via a locked gate at Struy. Permission and a key for the lock can be obtained by telephoning Struy 260, the cottage beside the gate. A stalkers' path climbs north into the corrie of Loch Toll a'Mhuic and on up the steep back wall of the corrie to finish just below the crest of Sgurr na Fearstaig. From here continue east to Sgurr Fhuar-thuill. The crest of the ridge is broad so follow the rim east, over the undulation of Creag Ghorm a'Bhealaich and down to the narrow saddle before Sgurr a'Choire Ghlais. Return to the main crest and descend to a saddle at the foot of Carn nan Ghobhar, from where an easy 400 ft/122 m climb leads to the stony summit. Continue east, then SE, and down into the Bealach nam Bogan then slopes to Sgurr na Ruaidhe.
Stalking Information: Broulin Estate Tel: Struy 260.

26 THE ACHNASHELLACH AND TORRIDON HILLS

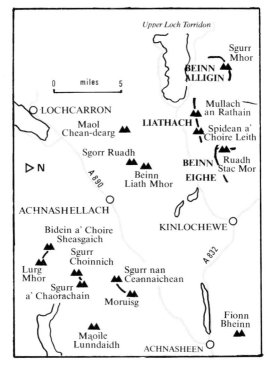

Upper Loch Torridon

Sgurr Mhor

BEINN ALLIGIN

0 miles 5

○ LOCHCARRON

Mullach an Rathain

LIATHACH

Maol Chean-dearg

Spidean a' Choire Leith

Sgorr Ruadh

BEINN EIGHE

Ruadh Stac Mor

▷ N

Beinn Liath Mhor

ACHNASHELLACH

KINLOCHEWE ○

Bidein a' Choire Sheasgaich

Sgurr Choinnich

Lurg Mhor

Sgurr nan Ceannaichean

Sgurr a' Chaorachain

Moruisg

Fionn Bheinn

Maoile Lunndaidh

ACHNASHEEN ○

Suggested Base:	Achnasheen or Torridon
Accommodation:	Hotels, guest houses and b/b at Achnasheen, Strathcarron, Torridon. Youth Hostels at Torridon. Private hostel at Craig, Achnashellach.
Public Transport:	Rail: Inverness to Kyle of Lochalsh. Stations at Achnasheen, Achnashellach and

Strathcarron. Buses: Inverness to Poolewe for Achnasheen and Kinlochewe, for onward post bus service. Post Buses: Achnasheen to Laide for Kinlochewe; Kinlochewe to Diabaig for Torridon.

Mountain: Moruisg, 3045 ft/928 m, Sgurr nan Ceannaichean, 3002 ft/915 m

Map: OS Sheet 25: GR 101499, GR 087481
Translation: big water, peak of the pedlars
Pronunciation: moarishk, skoor nan kyaneechan
Access Point: Glen Carron
Distance: 8 miles/3500 ft; 12.8 km/1067 m ascent
Approx Time: 4–6 hours
Route: Leave the A890 Glen Carron road at a car park about three-quarters of a mile west of the outflow of Loch Sgamhain. Cross the footbridge over the river and take a stalkers' path which runs up the east bank of the Alltan na Feola. After about 2.4 km leave the burn and climb east up grassy slopes. Continue until you reach the broad crest. Continue on the crest NE to the summit. Return and follow the broad ridge south over a subsidiary top and then descend more steeply SW to an obvious col. Climb west up a broad grassy ridge then SW after a distance to reach the flat summit of Sgurr nan Ceanaichean. The summit cairn overlooks the east corrie. Retrace your steps down the NE ridge then bear north down a steep ridge back to the Alltan na Feola.
Stalking Information: Glen Carron Estate.
Tel: Achnashellach 217.

Mountain: Maoile Lunndaidh, 3304 ft/1007 m, Sgurr a'Chaorachain, 3455 ft/1053 m, Sgurr Choinnich, 3277 ft/999 m

Map: OS Sheet 25: GR 135458, GR 087447, GR 076446
Translation: bare hill of the wet place, peak of the little field of the berries, moss peak

Fuar Tholl

Pronunciation: moela loondy, skoor a choerachan, skoor choanyeech
Access Point: Craig
Distance: 20 miles/5500 ft; 32 km/1676 m ascent
Approx Time: 8–12 hours
Route: Cross the railway and follow the Forestry Commission road, first parallel to the railway, then up through the forest to the locked gate at the top edge of the forest. Beyond the gate a path runs below the steep east face of Sgurr nan Ceanaichean and alongside the Allt a'Chonais. Continue on the track until it turns east towards distant Strathconon. Hereabouts a footbridge crosses the river and another track runs SW up and over the Bealach Bearnais. Follow this track a good distance up towards the bealach and then heading back east by way of the west ridge of Sgurr Choinnich. From the summit continue east across the flat summit and then down to the bealach before the long pull to Sgurr a'Chaorachain. Continue past the summit on broad slopes in an ESE direction towards Bidean an Eoin Deirg and from the bealach just before that summit, drop down steep slopes in a NE direction to reach the small lochan which lies at the foot of the west ridge of Carn nam Fiaclan. Ascend this ridge on to a broad tableland, cross the bealach at the head of Fuar-tholl Mor and cross a broad and featureless plateau in a NE direction to the large cairn on the summit of

Maoile Lunndaidh. Descend north along the east
rim of the Fuar-tholl Mor and down into Glean
Fhiodhaig. A path will take you west back to the
starting point.
Stalking Information: Achnashellach Estate.
Tel: Achnashellach 266.

Mountain: Bidein a'Choire Sheasgaich,
3100 ft/945 m, Lurg Mhor, 3235 ft/986 m

Map: OS Sheet 25: GR 049413, GR 165405
Translation: peak of the corrie of the milkless cattle,
big ridge stretching into the plain
Pronunciation: beetyan a chora haysgeech, loorak
voar
Access Point: Craig
Distance: 18 miles/5200 ft; 28.8 km/1585 m ascent
Approx Time: 8–12 hours
Route: From the footbridge over the Allt a'Chonais
follow the footpath to the summit of the Bealach
Bernais. From the boggy summit leave the path and
climb the NE ridge of Beinn Tharsuinn crossing
several undulations before reaching the summit.
Descend SW to a small lochan and then WSW to an
obvious col between the summit and the west top.
From here drop down steep slopes for a considerable
distance to reach the floor of the Bealach an
Sgoltaidh. Steep and craggy flanks guard Bidein
a'Choire Sheasgaich but an easier route can be found
by traversing slightly to the right and so avoiding the
steepest of the crags. A steep path zig-zags its way up
and you will top out beside a small lochan. Continue
south to the pointed summit of Sheasgaich. From the
summit descend south, then SE and follow the broad
ridge to Lurg Mhor. To return you have to retrace
your steps all the way to the Bealach Bearnais and the
Allt a'Chonais.
Stalking Information: Achnashellach Estate.
Tel: Achnashellach 266.

Mountain: Beinn Liath Mhor, 3035 ft/925 m, Sgorr
Ruadh, 3150 ft/960 m

Map: OS Sheet 25: GR 964520, GR 959504
Translation: big grey hill, red peak

Pronunciation: byn leea voar, skoor rooa
Access Point: Achnashellach
Distance: 9 miles/3750 ft; 14.4 km/1143 m ascent
Approx Time: 5–8 hours
Route: Take the path from Achnashellach station
through the pines above the River Lair. Climb above
the forest on the path to a heathery hillside beneath
the craggy terminal of Beinn Liath Mhor. Here the
path separates, with one path running NW into Coire
Lair and the other running NE into the Easan
Dorcha. Take the latter for a short distance to its
highest point, and then take the steep and unrelenting
heather slopes of Beinn Liath Mhor. Climb to its east
top and follow the stony quartzite ridge WNW to the
summit. Continue on the ridge, narrow in places and
descend to the Bealach Coire Lair, taking care as
there are some crags to bypass and a prominent knoll
either to cross, or circumnavigate. From the bealach
climb south on to the NW ridge of Sgurr Ruadh and
follow this ridge SE to the steep and prominent
summit. The descent SE is via the Bealach Mhoir and
wide open slopes back to the River Lair.
Stalking Information: Achnashellach Estate.
Tel: Achnashellach 266.

Mountain: Maol Chean-dearg, 3061 ft/933 m

Map: OS Sheet 25: GR 924498
Translation: bald red head
Pronunciation: moel chan dyerak
Access Point: Coulags
Distance: 8 miles/3000 ft; 12.8 km/914 m ascent
Approx Time: 3–5 hours
Route: From Coulags follow the path on the east side
of Fionn-abhainn. Cross the bridge to the west side
after 2.4 km or so and continue past the ruined
cottage to the Clach nan Con-fionn. Shortly after
this take the path which bears off west and climb to
the col between Maol Chean-dearg and Meall nan
Ceapairean. Turn NW here and climb the broad ridge
to the summit.
Stalking Information: Achnashellach Estate.
Tel: Achnashellach 266.

Mountain: Fionn Bheinn, 3061 ft/933 m

Map: OS Sheets 20 and 25: GR 147621
Translation: pale coloured hill
Pronunciation: fyoon vyn
Access Point: Achnasheen
Distance: 4 miles/3000 ft; 6.4 km/914 m ascent
Approx Time: 3–5 hours
Route: Follow the Allt Achadh na Sine from
Achnasheen and keep to its NE bank. Follow the
burn high up into a corrie west of Creagan nan Laogh
and climb grassy slopes north to the ridge. Follow the
ridge west to the summit.
Stalking Information: Loch Rosque Estate. Tel:
Achnasheen 266.

Beinn Alligin

Mountain: Beinn Alligin, 3232 ft/985 m

Map: OS Sheets 19 and 24: GR 866613
Translation: jewelled hill

Pronunciation: byn alligin
Access Point: Coire Mhic Nobuil bridge car park
Distance: 6 miles/3800 ft; 9.6 km/1158 m ascent
Approx Time: 4–6 hours
Route: Cross the road and take the path which crosses the moorland towards Coir' nan Laoigh of Tom na Gruagaich. Climb to the head of the corrie and ascend Tom na Gruagaich itself. Descend north down a rocky ridge to a col beyond which the ridge becomes broader. Climb NNE over a knoll, drop a little height to a bealach and then climb NE to Sgurr Mhor, the summit of Beinn Alligin. From here descend steeply ENE then east down a narrow ridge to a col. Follow the well-marked path over the Horns of Alligin, using hands as well as feet in places. From the third 'Horn' continue the descent SE to the moorland and the track in Coire Mhic Nobuil is joined.
Stalking Information: National Trust for Scotland. Tel: Torridon 221.

Mountain: Beinn Eighe (Ruadh-stac Mor), 3314 ft/1010 m

Map: OS Sheets 19 and 25: GR 951611
Translation: File hill, (big red peak)
Pronunciation: byn ay
Access Point: Car park on A896
Distance: 10 miles/3200 ft; 16 km/975 m ascent
Approx Time: 4–6 hours
Route: Leave the car park and follow the broad track which leads up Coire Dubh Mor. At GR 934594 take another path which runs north round the prow of Sail Mor and traverses the hillside before climbing up into Coire Mhic Fhearchair. Cross the outflow of the loch and follow the east side of the loch before climbing screes and rough slopes SE to reach the ridge which leads to the summit, Ruadh-stac Mor. The traverse of Beinn Eighe can be continued to take in Coinneach Mhor, Spidean Coire nan Clach and along the main ridge to Sgurr Ban and Sgurr nan Fhir Duibhe.
Stalking Information: Nature Conservancy Council. Tel: Kinlochewe 254.

Liathach

Mountain: Liathach, Spidean a'Choire Leith,
3458 ft/1054 m, Mullach an Rathain, 3356 ft/1023 m

Map: OS Sheet 25: GR 929580, GR 912577
Translation: grey one; peak of the grey corrie,
summit of the row of pinnacles
Pronunciation: leeahach, speetyan a chora lay,
moolach an raahan
Access Point: A896, half mile east of Glen Cottage
Distance: 7 miles/4300 ft; 11.2 km/1311 m ascent
Approx Time: 5–8 hours
Route: Leave the road just east of Glen Cottage
and climb steeply up the craggy hillside into the
Toll a'Meitheach. Higher up the corrie climb up
rightwards, NE, over steep ground to the col on the
main ridge. Follow the ridge NW then west over two
small tops to the cone of Spidean a'Choire Leith.
Descend SW to a short and level grassy section.
Continue over, or around the pinnacles of Am
Fasarinen. A path avoids the difficulties on the south
side. Beyond the pinnacles it is an easy stroll on to
Mullach an Rathain. From the summit the most
interesting descent back to Glen Torridon is via the
SW ridge.
Stalking Information: National Trust for Scotland.
Tel: Torridon 221.

27 THE DUNDONNELL AND FISHERFIELD HILLS

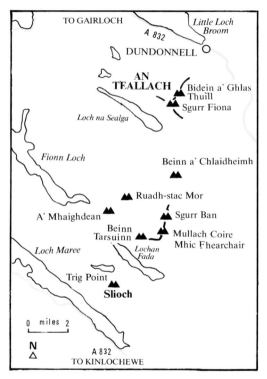

Suggested Base:	Kinlochewe or Dundonnell
Accommodation:	Hotels, b/b in Kinlochewe, Poolewe, Dundonnell. Private hostel at Sail Mhor, Dundonnell. Caravan site at Kinlochewe. Camping/caravan site at Gairloch

Public Transport:	Rail: Inverness to Kyle of Lochalsh – nearest stations at Garve and Achnasheen for onward bus services. Buses: Inverness to Poolewe for Kinlochewe. Inverness to Braemore and Gairloch for Dundonnell.

Mountain: Slioch, 3215 ft/980 m

Map: OS Sheet 19: GR 005688
Translation: from Gaelic sleagh, a spear
Pronunciation: Slee-och
Access Point: Incheril, Kinlochewe
Distance: 12 miles/3500 ft; 19.2 km/1067 m ascent
Approx Time: 6–9 hours
Route: Take the Incheril turn-off, east of Kinlochewe. From the road end follow the path which runs along the north bank of the Kinlochewe River. After 4.8 km cross the Abhainn an Fhasaigh and turn right on the path which runs up Gleann Bianasdail. After 0.8 km branch left on the well worn path which climbs north towards Slioch's SE corrie. Continue to gain the SE ridge and continue to the summit of Sgurr an Tuill Bhain. From here follow the ridge which leads to the north top then across a slight depression south to gain the summit. Descend by the SE ridge.
Stalking Information: Kinlochewe Estate.
Tel: Kinlochewe 262.

Mountain: Ruadh Stac Mor, 3012 ft/918 m, A'Mhaighdean, 3173 ft/967 m

Map: OS Sheet 19: GR 018756, GR 008749
Translation: big red peak, the maiden
Pronunciation: Roo-a stak more, ah-vtyin
Access Point: Poolewe
Distance: 25 miles/3900 ft; 40 km/1189 m ascent
Approx Time: 10–14 hours
Route: A private road leaves Poolewe and runs along the east side of the River Ewe to Inveran and

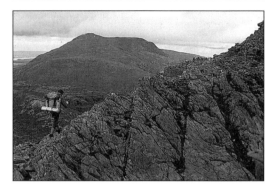

A'Mhaighdean

Kernsary. (Tel: Poolewe 346 for permission and key to drive as far as Kernsary.) From Kernsary go east then SE through forest to reach the path on the north bank of the Allt na Creige. This path is indistinct in places but soon descends to pass Loch an Doire Chrionaich. Continue south to cross Strathan Buidhe then continue to SE end of Fionn Loch. Cross the causeway between Fionn Loch and Dubh Loch and follow stalkers' path to Carnmore. Continue east, cross the Allt Bruthach an Easain and traverse SE across the hillside to reach the NW ridge of A'Mhaighdean. Follow the craggy ridge to the summit. From here descend NE to the grassy col below Ruadh Stac Mor. Climb the sandstone crags in a northerly direction to the summit trig point. Return to the col and take the stalkers' path to Carnmore and the return journey to Poolewe.
Stalking Information: Inveran Estate or Scatwell Estate. Tel: Poolewe 274 or Scatwell 230.

Mountain: Beinn a'Chlaidheimh, 2999 ft/914 m, Sgurr Ban, 3245 ft/989 m, Mullach Coire Mhic Fhearchair, 3343 ft/1019 m, Beinn Tarsuinn, 3071 ft/936 m

Map: OS Sheet 19: GR 061775, GR 055745, GR 052735, GR 039727

Translation: hill of the sword, light-coloured peak, summit of the corrie of Farquhar's son, transverse hill
Pronunciation: byn a'shleev, skoor bawn, moolach mora veechk erachar, byn tarshin
Access Point: Shenavall
Distance: 13 miles/5800 ft; 20.8 km/1768 m ascent
Approx Time: 8–12 hours
Route: From the bothy at Shenavall (GR 066810) cross the Abhainn Strath na Sealga. (Take care; the crossing of this river when in spate is not advisable and there is no bridge.) Climb the steep heather-covered slopes of Beinn a'Chlaidheimh to the SW. The slope becomes steeper as you reach the summit ridge and the final pull is up the ridge just east of the summit. Descend to the south on long scree slopes towards Loch a'Bhrisidh and follow the corrie rim to the summit of Sgurr Ban over acres of white quartzite scree. Continue to another scree filled col just south of Sgurr Ban where another steep climb takes you to the summit of Mullach Coire Mhic Fhearchair. Continue south to a prominent knob where the mountain's south ridge suddenly turns west to Beinn Tarsuinn. This can be turned by easy slopes to the east and south. Continue over rocky platforms to the summit of Beinn Tarsuinn. To return to Shenevall take a line across the north slopes to reach the stalkers' path in Gleann na Muice.
Stalking Information: Eilean Darach Estate. Tel: Dundonnell 202.

Mountain: An Teallach, Sgurr Fiona, 3474 ft/1059 m, Bidein a'Ghlas Thuill, 3484 ft/1062 m

Map: OS Sheet 19: GR 064837, GR 069844
Translation: the forge, peak of wine, peak of the greenish-grey hollow
Pronunciation: an tyalach, skoor fee-ana, beetyan a ghlas hil
Access Point: Dundonnell
Distance: 13 miles/5200 ft; 20.8 km/1585 m ascent
Approx Time: 6–10 hours
Route: Leave the A832 road about 500 metres SE of the hotel and follow the path which zig-zags up the

An Teallach: Sgurr Fiona (right) and the pinnacles

steep shoulder of Meall Garbh. The path disappears
around the 750 m contour so follow the broad stony
ridge south over a prominent knoll to another knoll
from where a short ascent ESE takes you to an
unnamed top at the edge of Glas Tholl. Descend
south to a col and then follow the easy ridge to the
summit of Bidein a'Ghlas Thuill. Descend SSW to a
col and then climb the steep and rocky ridge to the
summit of Sgurr Fiona. For a more interesting
descent follow the line of the SE ridge past (or over if
you don't mind an exposed scramble) the imposing
Lord Berkeley's Seat and the Corrag Bhuidhe
pinnacles to Sail Liath. Continue SE on the ridge to
reach the cairned path which runs from Shenavall to
Dundonnell.
***Stalking Information*:** Eilean Darach Estate.
Tel: Dundonnell 202. Dundonnell Estate. Tel:
Dundonnell 219.

28 FANNICHS AND ULLAPOOL HILLS

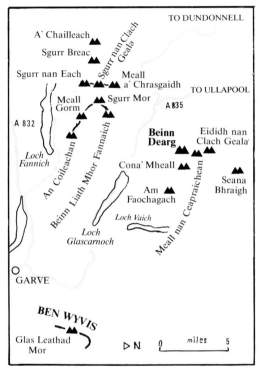

Suggested Base:	Garve or Ullapool
Accommodation:	Hotels, guest houses and b/b at Garve, Ullapool, Oykel Bridge and Aultguish. Youth Hostel at Ullapool. Camping/caravan sites at Ullapool and Garve
Public Transport:	Rail: Inverness to Kyle of Lochalsh. Station at Garve for

onward bus services. Buses:
Inverness to Gairloch for Garve,
Garbat, Aultguish, Dirrie More
and Braemore. Inverness to
Ullapool for Garve, Garbat,
Aultguish, Dirrie More and
Inverlael. Lairg to Lochinver for
Oykel Bridge (for Strath Mulzie).

Mountain: An Coileachan, 3028 ft/923 m, Meall
Gorm, 3113 ft/949 m, Sgurr Mor, 3645 ft/1111 m,
Beinn Liath Mhor Fannaich, 3130 ft/954 m, Meall
a'Chrasgaidh, 3064 ft/934 m, Sgurr nan Clach Geala,
3586 ft/1093 m, Sgurr nan Each, 3028 ft/923 m

Map: OS Sheet 20: GR 241680, GR 221696,
GR 203718, GR 219724, GR 184733, GR 184715,
GR 184697
Translation: the little cock, blue hill, big peak, big
grey hill of Fannich, hill of the crossing, peak of the
white stones, peak of the horses
Pronunciation: an kilyachan, myowl gorram, skoor
more, byn leea voar fannich, myowl a chraskee,
skoor nan klach gyala, skoor nan yach
Access Point: Fannich Lodge, GR 218660
Distance: 15 miles/6500 ft; 24 km/1981 m ascent
Approx Time: 8–12 hours
Route: Permission can be gained to drive from
Grudie bridge to Fannich Lodge, a distance of seven
miles (11.2 km). Telephone the Hydro Board, Grudie
Power Station Garve 209. From Fannich Lodge climb
the slopes of An Coileachan from where a broad ridge
stretches in a NW direction to Meall Gorm where two
tops appear as little more than the high spots on a
broad and featureless ridge. The true summit is the
one with a wind break shelter built near it. Continue
over the long pull to Meall nam Peithirean and
onwards towards Sgurr Mor. Just before the final rise
to the summit of Sgurr Mor, however, a ridge breaks
off east to the summit of Beinn Liath Mhor Fannaich.
Return to Sgurr Mor and continue NW to Carn na
Chriche and Meall a'Chrasgaidh. Leave the summit

Sgurr Mor, Fannich

in a southerly direction, cross the saddle of Am
Biachdiach and climb the steep and rocky NNE ridge
of Sgurr nan Clach Geala. Continue easily south to
Sgurr nan Each and then south and SE to the track
beside Loch Fannich.
Stalking Information: Eastern Munros –
Kinlochluichart Estate. Tel: Garve 228. Western
Munros – Fannich Estate. Tel: Almondbank 236.

Mountain: A'Chailleach, 3277 ft/999 m, Sgurr Breac, 3281 ft/1000 m

---

Map: OS Sheets 19 and 20: GR 136714, GR 158711
Translation: the old woman, speckled peak
Pronunciation: a chalyach, skoor brechk
Access Point: A832 near Loch a'Bhraoin
Distance: 10 miles/3750 ft; 16 km/1143 m ascent
Approx Time: 5–8 hours
Route: Take the private road to Loch a'Bhraoin. Cross its outlet and continue on the stalkers' path beside the Allt Breabaig in a southerly direction as far as the high bealach which leads over to Loch Fannich. From the pass climb the east ridge of Sgurr Breac. Continue by traversing Toman Coinich and descending to the col below its west slopes. Follow the rim of the corrie Toll an Lochain to its junction with the Sron na Goibhre spur then continue SW along a gently rising ridge to the summit of A'Chailleach.
Stalking Information: Fannich Estate.
Tel: Almondbank 236.

Mountain: Ben Wyvis, Glas Leathad Mor, 3432 ft/1046 m

Map: OS Sheet 20: GR 463684
Translation: from Gaelic fuathas – possibly hill of terror, big greenish grey slope
Pronunciation: byn wivis, glas lehat moar
Access Point: Garbat
Distance: 14 miles/4300 ft; 22.4 km/1311 m ascent
Approx Time: 6–10 hours
Route: Take the muddy track which runs alongside the Allt a' Bhealaich Mhoir. Continue past the forest plantation and turn uphill to climb the steep slopes of An Cabar. From the top the summit lies just over a mile in a NE direction over a rolling mossy ridge.
Stalking Information: Mountgarret Estate.
Tel: Evanton 645.

Mountain: Am Faochagach, 3130 ft/954 m

Map: OS Sheet 20: GR 304794
Translation: place of the shells
Pronunciation: am foechakach
Access Point: A835 NW end of Loch Glascarnoch
Distance: 9 miles/2300 ft; 14.4 ft/701 m ascent
Approx Time: 4–6 hours
Route: Start at the bridge over the Abhainnan an Torrain Dubh. Cross the moorland in an easterly direction passing between Loch Glascarnoch and Loch a'Gharbhrain. The crossing of the Abhainn a'Gharbhrain will entail wading to a greater or lesser degree depending on the weather conditions. Once across the river turn NE and climb the steep heather slopes to reach the main ridge just south of the summit. From there the going is easy along a broad and obvious ridge.
Stalking Information: Braemore Estate. Tel: Loch Broom 255.

Mountain: Beinn Dearg, 3556 ft/1084 m, Cona'Mheall, 3215 ft/980 m, Meall nan Ceapraichean, 3205 ft/977 m, Eididh nan Clach Geala, 3045 ft/928 m

Map: OS Sheet 20: GR 259812, GR 275816, GR 257826, GR 257843
Translation: red hill, hill of the joining, possibly from ceap, meaning a rounded hilltop, web of the white stones
Pronunciation: byn dyerak, konival, myowl nan kyapreechan, aydyee nan klach gyala
Access Point: Inverlael
Distance: 15 miles/5000 ft; 24 km/1524 m ascent
Approx Time: 7–11 hours
Route: Take the private road through the forest into Gleann na Squaib. Follow the stalkers' path up the glen to the broad saddle at its head. From the saddle go south by a massive drystone dyke and follow it up Beinn Dearg's north ridge. Where the dyke turns west go through a gap and cross the bald summit dome in a SSW direction to the cairn. Return to the saddle and climb the easy angled ridge to the east to Cona'

Mheall. Return to the saddle and climb the broad SE ridge of Meall nan Ceapraichean. Continue NE along a broad stony ridge to Ceann Garbh, descend NE down rocky and craggy slopes to another col at the foot of Eididh nan Clach Geala's SE ridge. Climb the easy grassy ridge to the top where the NW cairn is the summit. Descend west down grassy slopes for a short distance then go SW into the corrie west of Lochan na Chnapaich where a path leads downhill to the main path in Gleann na Squaib.

Stalking Information: Inverlael estate. Tel: Loch Broom 262.

Mountain: Seana Bhraigh, 3041/927 m

Map: OS Sheet 20: GR 281879
Translation: old upper part
Pronunciation: shena vry
Access Point: Inverlael
Distance: 16 miles/3700 ft; 25.6 km/1128 m ascent
Approx Time: 7–10 hours
Route: From Inverlael follow the forest track as far as Glensquaib. Continue by the stalkers' track which leads out of the forest and on to the Druim na Saobhaidhe ridge. From this ridge cross the wide corrie of Gleann a'Mhadaidh and round a spur of hills above to continue up Coire an Lochain Sgeirich. Continue across boggy terrain towards Loch a'Chadha Dheirg from where a northerly direction will take you to the easy slopes to the SW top. From there follow the cliff edge to the summit of Seana Bhraigh.

Stalking Information: Inverlael Estate. Tel: Loch Broom 262.

29 ASSYNT AND THE FAR NORTH

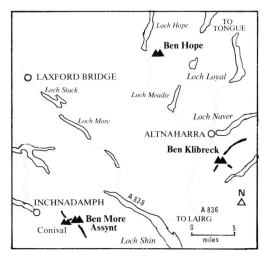

Suggested Base:	Lairg, Altnaharra or Inchnadamph
Accommodation:	Hotels at Altnaharra, Crask Inn, Tongue, Lairg and Inchnadamph. Youth Hostels at Durness and Tongue. Camping/caravan sites at Lairg and Tongue.
Public Transport:	Rail: Inverness to Wick and Thurso. Station at Lairg for onward post bus. Buses: Inverness to Wick and Thurso for Bonar Bridge; Inverness to Dornoch for Bonar Bridge; Bonar Bridge to Lairg; Lairg to Lochinver for Inchnadamph; Thurso to Tongue. Post Buses:

Lairg to Talmine for Crask Inn
(Klibreck). Altnaharra to
Portnacon and Rispond for
Atnacallich.

Mountain: Ben More Assynt, 3274 ft/998 m,
Conival, 3238 ft/987 m

Map: OS Sheet 15: GR 318201, GR 303199
Translation: big hill of Assynt, hill of joining
Pronunciation: byn moar assint, konival
Access Point: Inchnadamph
Distance: 11 miles/3700 ft; 17.6 km/1128 m ascent
Approx Time: 4–7 hours
Route: Take the farm track, just north of the
Inchnadamph Hotel, which runs alongside the River
Traligill. Follow the path to the Traligill Caves, but
stay on the NE bank. Opposite the caves leave the
track and take to the slopes on the SW face of Beinn
an Fhurain. Aim for the obvious col between Beinn
an Fhurain and Conival. From the col the final slopes
lead to a level ridge and the summit. Continue east for
a mile along the rough ridge of scree and crag to the
summit of Ben More Assynt. The summit cairn is on
the north top.
Stalking Information: Inchnadamph Estate.
Tel: Lochinver 203.

Mountain: Ben Klibreck, 3153 ft/961 m

Map: OS Sheet 16: GR 585299
Translation: hill of the speckled cliff
Pronunciation: byn kleebreck
Access Point: A836 Lairg/Tongue road, GR 545303
Distance: 7 miles/2600 ft; 11.2 km/792 m ascent
Approx Time: 4–6 hours
Route: Cross the river (no footbridge) and go east
across the moorland towards Loch nan Uan. From
the north end of the loch go SE up steep grassy slopes
to the main ridge. Follow the easy ridge to a bouldery
slope which leads to the summit.
Stalking Information: Altnaharra Estate.
Tel: Altnaharra 220.

Ben Hope

Mountain: Ben Hope, 3041 ft/927 m

Map: OS Sheet 9:
Translation: hill of the bay
Pronunciation: byn hope
Access Point: Alltnacaillich
Distance: 4 miles/3000 ft; 6.4 km/914 m ascent
Approx Time: 2–4 hours
Route: From the farm at Alltnacaillich go north for a mile and leave the road by a sheep shed. Follow the stream and head NE to make for an obvious break in the crags which takes you on to a wide terrace above the escarpment. Turn north and follow the cliff edge which buttresses the mountain's summit.
Stalking Information: Eriboll Estate. Tel: Altnaharra 248.

30 SKYE AND MULL

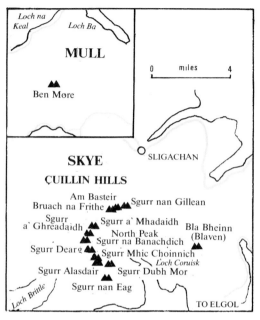

Suggested Base:	Glen Brittle (Skye)
Accommodation:	Hotels, guest houses and b/b at Broadford, Portree, Sligachan and Carbost. Youth Hostels at Broadford and Glen Brittle. Camp site at Glen Brittle.
Public Transport:	Rail: Inverness to Kyle of Lochalsh and Glasgow to Mallaig for ongoing ferries and bus services. Buses: Glasgow and Fort William to Uig. Edinburgh and Perth to Portree. Inverness to Portree. Portree to Fiskavaig for Sligachan and Carbost

	(nearest village to Glen Brittle). Armadale to Kyleakin for Broadford. Post Bus: Broadford to Elgol for Loch Slapin.
Suggested Base:	Tobermory (Mull)
Accommodation:	Hotels, guest houses and b/b at Tobermory. Youth Hostel.
Public Transport:	Ferry: Oban to Craignure. Buses: Craignure to Tobermory.

Blaven and Clach Glas

Mountain: Bla Bheinn (Blaven) 3045 ft/928 m

Map: OS Sheet 32: GR 530217
Translation: possibly blue hill, or possibly warm hill
Pronunciation: blaavin
Access Point: Head of Loch Slapin
Distance: 4 miles/3100 ft; 6.4 km/9.45 m ascent
Approx Time: 2–5 hours
Route: Leave the Elgol road at the Allt na Dunaiche just south of the head of Loch Slapin on its west side. Take the path that runs alongside the north bank of the stream through a wooded gorge, and then more steeply into Coire Uaigneich. Here the path becomes indistinct in places, but turns NNW up a steep slope just right of an obvious gully and soon reaches on to a distinct shoulder. Once this shoulder abuts on to the

main ridge follow it in a WSW direction, following
the rim of the ridge. As you climb closer to the
summit dome there are one or two rocky obstacles to
be scrambled over before more scree slopes lead to the
summit.
Stalking Information: Strathaird Estate.
Tel: Loch Scavaig 232.

Mountain: Sgurr Dubh Mor, 3097 ft/944 m, Sgurr
nan Eag 3037 ft/924 m

Map: OS Sheet 32: GR 457205, GR 457195
Translation: big black peak, peak of the notches
Pronunciation: skoor doo moar, skoor nan ayg
Access Point: Glen Brittle House
Distance: 9 miles/3900 ft; 14.4 km/1189 m ascent
Approx Time: 4–6 hours
Route: From the camp site in Glen Brittle follow the
track towards Coire Lagan but after half a mile or so
leave the path and cross the moorland in an ESE
direction towards Sron na Ciche. Make for the edge
of Coir' a'Ghrunnda by contouring around the foot
of Sron na Ciche, and then climb into the corrie to
reach the lochan. From the lochan climb easy slopes
which lead to an obvious col on the main ridge
between Sgurr Dubh na Da Bheinn and Sgurr
Thearlaich. Climb easy slopes to Sgurr Dubh na Da
Bheinn and from there follow the ridge east to Sgurr
Dubh Mor. Return to Sgurr Dubh na Da Bheinn and
descend south along the main ridge, traversing below
the steep-sided Caisteal a'Garbh-choire on either its
west or east side. Continue along the main ridge to
Sgurr nan Eag.

Mountain: Sgurr Alasdair, 3258 ft/993 m, Sgurr
Mhic Choinnich, 3110 ft/948 m
Inaccessible Pinnacle, 3235 ft/986 m

Map: OS Sheet 32: GR 449208, GR 450210, GR 444215
Translation: Alexander's Peak (named after Sheriff
Alexander Nicolson who made the first ascent in
1873), MacKenzie's Peak (named after John
Mackenzie the first Skye guide), inaccessible pinnacle
Pronunciation: skoor alastar, skoor veechk chunyeech

Access Point: Glen Brittle
Distance: 9 miles/5500 ft; 14.4 km/1676 m ascent
Approx Time: 6–8 hours
Route: Sgurr Alasdair by way of the Sron na Ciche above Coir' a'Ghrunnda. This involves a section between Sgurr Sgumain and Sgurr Alasdair which involves some climbing of a difficult standard, but that can be avoided by going a few yards towards the Coir' a'Ghrunnda side of the ridge where a short chimney offers an easier scramble back to the main ridge and to the summit. From here descend to the gap between Alasdair and Sgurr Thearlaich, and scramble up the latter's southern rib to the summit. Abseiling is usually required to reach the gap before Sgurr Mhic Choinnich. From here move up a little and then traverse round the west face by Collie's Ledge (moderate difficulty – rock climbing). A much more direct route for climbers takes the obvious corner of King's Chimney (difficult) on the south side. Walkers who don't wish to climb are best descending to Coire Lagan by the Great Stone Chute between Sgurr Alasdair and Sgurr Thearlaich, regaining the ridge by the An Stac screes. From the summit of Sgurr Mhic Choinnich descend NNE to the col above the An Stac screes. It will be necessary to drop down a little to reach a cairned path in the scree which leads up below the west edge of An Stac's tower. Staying close to the base of its wall climb to easier ground. Continue on the main ridge and climb the Inaccessible Pinnacle by its east ridge (moderate difficulty – rock climbing). On the tiny summit a convenient boulder provides an anchor for a 60 foot/18 m abseil off the west side of the pinnacle. Descend to Glen Brittle by Sgurr Dearg's west ridge.

Mountain: Sgurr na Banachdich, 3166 ft/965 m, Sgurr a'Chreadaidh, 3192 ft/973 m, Sgurr a'Mhadaidh, 3012 ft/918 m

---

Map: OS Sheet 32: GR 440225, GR 445232, GR 446235
Translation: possibly smallpox peak, peak of torment, peak of the fox
Pronunciation: skoor na banachteech, skoor a ghraytee, skoor a vaady

Access Point: Glen Brittle
Distance: 9 miles/4400 ft; 14.4 km/1341 m ascent
Approx Time: 4–6 hours
Route: Take the path above the Eas Mor waterfalls to
the upper basin of Coire na Banachdich. From here a
cairned route takes a devious line beneath the crags of
Sgurr Dearg eventually turning left to reach screes
which lead to a gap in the ridge north of Sgurr Dearg.
To the north, across the Bealach Coire na
Banachdich, steep rock and screes lead to Sron
Bhuidhe, then two more 'tops' before the final pull to
Sgurr na Banachdich. From the summit a short dip
leads to the foot of Sgurr Thormaid. This is climbed
by scrambling over large blocks and boulders. From
the summit continue to the NE avoiding the 'three
teeth' by traversing easy angled slabs on their left.
Follow the short narrow arête which leads to a
400 foot/122 m scramble on good holds to the south
top of Sgurr a'Ghreadaidh. Follow the very narrow
ridge crest to the summit. Continue on the narrow
ridge down into the gap known as the Eag Dubh. This
is followed by another descent to a second gap, the
An Dorus. From here scramble to the SW summit of
Sgurr a'Mhadaidh, the only 'top' which is given
Munro status. Follow the ridge NW which runs out to
Sgurr Thuilm and drop down into Coire an Durus
from the obvious col, returning to Glen Brittle.

Mountain: Sgurr nan Gillean, 3166 ft/965 m, Am
Basteir, 3068 ft/935 m, Bruach na Frithe,
3143 ft/958 m

Map: OS Sheet 32: GR 472253, GR 465253, GR 461252
Translation: peak of the young men, meaning
obscure, slope of the deer forest
Pronunciation: skoor nan geelyan, am bastar,
brooach na freea
Access Point: Sligachan
Distance: 9 miles/3800 ft; 14.4 km/1158 m ascent
Approx Time: 4–7 hours
Route: A footpath leaves the Carbost road just
beyond the Sligachan Hotel and leads to an old power
house. A nearby bridge crosses a stream and a
footpath crosses the moor towards the foot of Sgurr

nan Gillean's northern flank. Follow this path as far
as the Allt Dearg Beag. From here continue on the
west bank of the stream to a bridge. Cross the stream
and follow the path which heads in a southerly
direction. Continue into Coire Riabhach past the
lochan with the obvious wall of the Pinnacle Ridge on
your right. A long, hard pull through a jumble of
boulders eventually gives access to the crest of the SE
ridge. The ridge is at first fairly broad, but higher up it
narrows considerably and you will have to scramble
the final few feet to the summit of Sgurr nan Gillean.
Descend the west ridge steeply to the Tooth of Sgurr
nan Gillean. To the north of the Tooth a narrow cleft
known as Nicholson's Chimney offers an abseil route
to the base of the crag from where you can contour
across the screes to regain the ridge east of Am
Basteir. An easy but exposed scramble leads to the
summit. Descend to the Bhasteir Tooth by way of
ledges on the Lota Corrie (south) side for
60 feet/18 m. Here the way down is made difficult by a
small wall. Either abseil or descend a difficult pitch of
about 20 feet/six metres down a slightly easier-angled
section of wall to the SE. From the foot of the wall a
sloping shelf and ramp leads to the top of the Bhasteir
Tooth. From here abseil down the line of Naismith's
Route to the Bealach nan Lice, or alternatively,
return to the wall which you climbed earlier or
abseiled down, and follow a terrace which inclines
down towards Lota Corrie. Narrow shelves and walls
lead to wider ledges at the foot of the cliffs from
where you can climb screes up to the Bealach nan
Lice. From the bealach climb over Sgurr a'Fionn
Choire to reach Bruach na Frithe. Descend by the
NW ridge to the Bealach a'Mhaim and Sligachan.

Mountain: Ben More (Mull) 3169 ft/966 m

Map: OS Sheet 48: GR 526331
Translation: big hill
Pronunciation: byn moar
Access Point: Loch na Keal
Distance: 8 miles/3100 ft; 12.8 km/945 m ascent
Approx Time: 4–7 hours
Route: Start at the foot of the Abhainn na h-Uamha

and follow the south bank up the grassy Gleann na Beinne Fada to reach the col between Beinn Fhada and A'Chioch. Turn south and climb towards A'Chioch. Continue on the ridge over A'Chioch to Ben More. Descend by the broad NW ridge.
Stalking Information: Knock Estate. Tel: Aros 410.

RECOMMENDED BOOKS

Bennet, Donald (ed), *The Munros: the Scottish Mountaineering Club Hillwalkers' Guide*, Glasgow, Scottish Mountaineering Trust, 1985.

Brown, Hamish, *Hamish's Mountain Walk: the first traverse of all the Scottish Munros in one journey*, London, Gollancz, 1978.

Butterfield, Irvine, *The High Mountains of Britain and Ireland*, London, Diadem Books, 1986.

Gilbert, Richard, *Memorable Munros*, Leicester, Diadem Books, 1983.

Moran, Martin, *The Munros in Winter: 277 summits in 83 days*, Newton Abbot, David and Charles, 1986.

Mountaineering Council of Scotland and the Scottish Landowners' Federation (compilers), *Heading for the Scottish Hills*, Glasgow, Scottish Mountaineering Trust, 1988.

Munro's Tables of the 3000-feet mountains of Scotland and other tables of lesser heights, Revised edn, Edinburgh, Scottish Mountaineering Trust, 1984.

Weather information
Climber and hillwalker climblines:

East Highlands,   Tel: 0898 654 668
West Highlands,   Tel: 0890 654 669

INDEX OF MUNROS
IN ORDER OF HEIGHT

79	Sgurr Fhuar-thuill	25	107
80	Creag Mhor	7	29
81	Carn an t-Sagairt Mor	18	72
82	Chno Dearg	13	55
83	Ben Wyvis – Glas Leathad Mor	28	124
84	Cruach Ardrain	2	16
85	Beinn Iutharn Mhor	17	68
86	Stob Coir' an Albannaich	10	38
87	Meall nan Tarmachan	6	27
88	Carn Mairg	5	23
89	Sgurr na Ciche	23	93
90	Meall Chaordie	7	29
91	Beinn Achaladair	8	33
92	Sgurr a'Bhealaich Dheirg	24	101
93	Carn a'Mhaim	20	82
94	Gleoraich	23	96
95	Carn Dearg	14	58
96	Am Bodach	11	48
97	Beinn Fhada (Ben Attow)	25	104
98	Carn an Righ	17	68
99	Ben Oss	3	19
100	Carn Gorm	5	23
101	Sgurr a Mhaoraich	23	96
102	Sgurr na Ciste Duibhe	24	100
103	Ben Challum	7	30
104	Sgorr Dearg – Beinn a'Bheithir	10	45
105	Liathach – Mullach an Rathain	26	115
106	Buchaille Etive Mor – Stob Dearg	10	42
107	Aonach air Chrith	24	99
108	Ladhar Bheinn	23	95
109	Mullach Coire Mhic Fhearchair	27	118
110	BeinnBheoil	14	59
111	Mullach Clach a'Bhlair	19	77
112	Carn an Tuirc	18	71
113	Garbh Chioch Mhor	23	93
114	Cairn Bannoch	18	73
115	Beinn Ime	1	13
116	Sgurr an Doire Leathain	24	99
117	Beinn Eighe – Ruadh-stac Mor	26	114

161	Ben Vorlich (Loch Earn)	4	21
162	An Gearanach	11	48
163	Ciste Dubh	24	101
164	Mullach na Dheiragain	25	105
165	Stob Coire a'Chairn	11	48
166	Maol Chinn-dearg	24	99
167	Creag Mhor	5	23
168	Beinn a'Chochuill	9	35
169	Slioch – Trig Point	27	117
170	Cona' Mheall	28	125
171	Beinn Dubhcraig	3	19
172	Meall nan Ceapraichean	28	125
173	Stob Ban	12	52
174	Stob Coire Sgriodain	13	55
175	Beinn a'Ghlo – Carn Liath	16	65
176	Stuc a Chroin	4	21
177	Carn a'Gheoidh	17	68
178	A'Mharconaich	15	62
179	Ben Lomond	1	12
180	Beinn Sgritheall	23	95
181	Sgurr a'Chreadaidh	30	134
182	Meall Garbh	5	23
183	Aonach Eagach – Sgor nam Fiannaidh	10	44
184	A'Mhaighdean	27	117
185	Ben More – Mull	30	136
186	Sgurr na Banachdich – North Peak	30	134
187	Sgurr nan Gillean	30	135
188	Carn a'Chlamain	16	66
189	Sgurr Thuilm	22	91
190	Ben Klibreck	29	128
191	Sgorr Ruadh	26	111
192	Beinn nan Aighenan	10	37
193	Meall Glas	7	30
194	Stuchd an Lochain	5	24
195	Saileag	24	101
196	Beinn Fhionnlaidh	10	41
197	Buachaille Etive Beag – Stob Dubh	10	42
198	Bruach na Frithe	30	135
199	Tolmount	18	71
200	Tom Buidhe	18	71
201	Carn Ghluasaid	24	102
202	Sgurr nan Coireachan	22	91
203	Sgor Gaibhre	13	56